A book about two Black Americas, separate and unequal

When the racist looks like you
MEMOIR OF AN UNCLE TOM

Jimmie Pratt

ISBN: 979-8-218-27455-9 (Paperback)

Library of Congress Control Number: 2021921415

Printed by Diggy POD, Inc., in the United States of America.

First printing edition 2021.

KRAM 6:4 AM

Praymoore@yahoo.com

http://kram64.com

Published by KRAM 6:4 Adversary Media
KRAM is a palindrome for MARK, 6 is Chapter 4 is verse,
,” I knew what to expect”

I was 9 and hesitant to give up comic books. My mother handed me the novel, Peyton Place and told me the pictures are in your head.

This excerpt is from my mother's church biography: "…Just before my birthday, I got pregnant with my first child. This was the most unhappiest time of my life. After Jimmie was born, he was such a beautiful baby and so sweet. He trusted me, and he didn't care if I was tall and skinny. He was just sweet and he just love me to death. So I just worked hard and I took care of him…."

My children
Sonjii
Bryant
Akeshia

My sister Ann

My dear cousin Che Che

In Memoriam
My Nieces Michelle and Charlene

My Vietnam Brothers written as a shield against tyranny

The God Problem

On the seventh day, God rested. On that day, all the laws that govern physics and human behavior were fixed and in place. "In the beginning," Newton's Third Law of Motion, "For every action, there is an equal and opposite reaction," was God's first law of consequences... "whatsoever a man soweth, that shall he also reap."

From beginning to end, the Bible is filled with examples of humankind disobeying God's Laws. Doing so today is no less consequential. More often than not, disobedience is followed by wrathful judgment.

For more than 150 years, America has moved steadily towards a "more perfect union." Even after the passage of the Civil Rights Act of 1964, the Voting Rights Act, Affirmative Action, the emergence of a Black billionaire class, and a Black President, Black Americans, as a race, are still on the bottom rung of the social and economic ladder.

Despite all the progress, most African Americans prefer to use their voting power to push equity and settle for a "first Black" this or that person. LIBERAL African Americans do this even though they had the right to vote and became President and Vice President before White women, who are called privileged. Therefore, when Woke African Americans claim that Black people are the victims of systemic racism," the defeat of Jim Crow, the continuing existence of marginalized White women, and a Black man having occupied the White House makes a powerful argument for a more thorough explanation.

I will argue that the social, economic, and racial problems of Black people resulted from the Laws of Consequence. These laws are not to be confused with the law of unintended consequences. In contrast, the Laws of Consequence are tied to behavior like being ungrateful, abandoning their children, and returning to Pharaoh (the Democrat Party) without reverence to the Republican Party, which ended their bondage.

James Baldwin wrote about the Laws of Consequence in his book: *The Fire Next Time*. These are laws that deliver a judgment no police, army, or legislature can prevent. It is the retribution that follows "laws" we are all too familiar with. For every action, there's an equal and opposite action; "What goes around must come down. It is a promise based on certainty, and as ominous as the warning in the lyrics of an old Negro spiritual: "God gave Noah the rainbow sign, no more water, the fire next time." Therefore, the challenges facing Black Americans today and all the injustices of the past half-century are not the results of racism. It looks more like God just walked away.

Table of Content

Memoir of an Uncle Tom

The character Uncle Tom was created by abolitionist Harriet Beecher Stowe in 1852 to help free Black people from slavery. Today, the name is a derogatory term used to describe the world's best-known pediatric surgeon and a Supreme Court Justice. Dr. Carson and Justice Thomas are unwelcome and unwanted among the African American majority. Somehow the descendants of slaves have turned his name into a weapon to control the kind of runaways Uncle Tom dedicated himself to protecting.

I have to give the Democrat Party credit. Democrats know how to make both a slave and a racist. They have used that skill to turn African Americans into both. Using the same divisive "us against them" tactic they used to create the Ku Klux Klan, the Democrat Party gradually changed most African Americans into racist voting stock over the past half-century. This blind obedience by African American Progressives today provides a retrospective anthropological look into the making of a slave. From the passage of the Civil Rights Act of 1964 to the election of Joe Biden, the African American

Democrat vote has been the new cotton. This book documents this metamorphosis through the life of one man.

My memoir is not an autobiography. This book is a historical account of events in my life. As much as I hate disappointing my critics, this book is about betrayal, bigotry, and self-hate in a separate and unequal Black America.

This memoir, of an Uncle Tom as I'm called, unmasks a race of mostly "God-fearing" people living in ways that are contrary to their history of struggle and antithetical to their stated religious beliefs.

I argue that the people bought out of bondage along with their corrupt religious, social, and political leaders covered up racism, protected the Klan, and became a self-hate group. This book is their biography. They are the Sellouts and the face of White Supremacy. I am the person they are trying to silence by labeling me an Uncle Tom.

In August of 2021, Erika D Smith, a columnist for the LA Times, wrote the article: "Larry Elder is the Black face of White Supremacy, you've been warned." Most enlightened Americans know that her column was not news or written to inform. Ms. Smith sent out a Pavlovian wake-up call or dog whistle for African American voters to vote based on their hatred of Republicans rather than their interest. This was also the "wink, nod, and gun" or the OK for White Liberal racists to throw eggs at Larry Elder and show up in racist gorilla masks.

Although unintended, Ms. Smith's column underpins the basic claim I'm making with this book. By claiming Larry Elder is the face of "White Supremacy," Ms. Smith is admitting that African Americans are a vital part of the American racial construct. This memoir of an Uncle Tom not only identifies which Black Americans are the face of White Supremacy, but it also unveils the attacks on Conservatives as another slick campaign to disguise Jim Crow as equity.

Anytime Black Americans freely choose to think for themselves or vote differently, Jim Crow appears in the form of equity. Black Conservatives are then isolated, attacked, and sometimes killed by the "D.A.A.M." people (Democrat African American Majority).

Fake equity has turned the D.A.A.M. people into a woke Klan that wages war on Black people and White Conservatives. Together with Liberal White women, they have created an industry that exploits race, while abandoning every issue that is genuinely important to Black people. This warped ideological alliance not only made people like Stacy Abrams, Al Sharpton, and many others rich and powerful, this alliance gave birth to a racial industrial complex

After electing the Democrat nominee President in 2020, woke descendants of those who gave their lives for the right to vote, singlehandedly gave Democrats complete control of the national government. Moreover, they gave them an iron fist with which to control the government. In return, Democrats used the African American vote, the new cotton, to support illegal immigration, unlawful mandates, and the jailing of American citizens without due process. All of the evil done in the name of ending racism and

COVID was made possible by the African American vote. Political power that could have been used to educate Black kids gave rise to the same oppressive Jim Crow-era behavior that subjugated Black people in the past.

My memoir takes readers down the destructive path laid out by "Woke disobedient liberal African Americans." . Even before the sixes are passed out, they metaphorically invite the Horsemen of the Apocalypse into our lives The retribution that followed getting nothing in return gave birth to an ungodly social, religious, and political leadership class.

Each section of my book supports the claims made in this chapter, and demonstrates the role Woke African Americans play in maintaining White Supremacy in the two Black Americas. Before the end of this book, you will know just how far the D.A.A.M. people went to protect the interests of the Democrat Party, and pee on the graves of Malcolm and Martin in the process.

In a Bizarro World twist of fate, the leadership class that wokeness created got the African American majority to become the victims of what was supposed to be cures. The remedies African Americans came up with to end injustice and racism could have been created and implemented by the Ku Klux Klan. This waywardness and "backasswards" way of thinking have led to a new kind of exploitation made just for Black people. For example, after fighting to end "White Only" African Americans accepted separate graduations, and separate dorms. During COVID, they even accepted medical Apartheid, which will probably end up being the world's largest clinical trial.

Whether praying, protesting, or voting in record numbers for change, African American visits to the polls always lead to consequences and contradictions that don't benefit Black people. For example, African American Democrats claimed the police are murdering Black people. Not only do they elect a career policeman as mayor of New York City, but somehow politicians they elect are never responsible for the police hired by them. Somehow, this misguided protest over police conduct gave birth to BLM, a Godless, ruthless anti-family, Marxist organization they prayed into existence. And out of that came a Black Princess, Meghan Markle, and a Black First Lady, Michelle Obama, claiming to be oppressed people.

In return for their obedience, the Left defunded the Police, emptied the jails, banned bail, and gave African Americans a license to steal all in the name of equity. By so-called helping, the Left created more oppression and killings than they had accused the police and the Klan of committing. Caught in the crosshairs of this warped social justice movement are Black kids who need a healthy race, if they are to thrive. Instead of prayers and legislation, Black kids get equity. If Black kids cannot read, write, and do math, the solution has been to promote them anyway.

In another Bizarro World twist of fate, Woke African Americans, who use their Bibles as a crutch and weapons supported BLM's stated goal of ending the patriarchal family. As so-called Christians, they support gender selection and abortion on demand. When Sunday comes around, they condemn the things they voted for.

Transgressions like this led Black people into an apocalyptic dystopian hellhole where churches have become what Dr. King called "...Irrelevant social clubs with no real meaning..."

Hopefully, this memoir will end the weaponization of racism by providing people who are continuously attacked and labeled as racists with the ammunition to fight back. I hope and pray that my book will give rise to more Black Conservatives, even though the latter have been ostracized, called Uncle Tom, marginalized, and even killed to silence their voices. I also want this book to be the first draft of history, to ensure the right Black people are held responsible for the Black race's return to servitude.

If enough books like this one are written, history will hold the woke voting class of Black Americans responsible. The Democrat African American Majority used voting rights as a pretext to gain economic power for others and not themselves. They propped up politicians, entertainers, civil rights leaders, and preachers, who, in return, rob the Black race of the ability to think for themselves, nurture and protect Black children. History will also record that this voting class created the two Black Americas. This class is also responsible for Black people's inability to take advantage of what any illegal immigrant coming across the border sees.

Recognizing the two Black Americas will make the Black race more democratic. Woke African Americans will be held responsible for the social, political, and economic issues they created and now want a reparation check for. Life and death issues such as Black-on-Black violence, underperforming schools, poverty, and other issues that impact the Black community will no longer follow the laws of consequence but be of consequence.

When actual victims of racism are finally heard, Americans will know that the fight against this everything is racist, is a Ponzi scheme wrapped in a hoax and perpetrated on the American people. The American people will see how they have been blinded by "a well-packaged web of lies," to quote Dresden. These lies, disguised as news, have allowed one group of people to believe the color black is a franchise owned by the Democrat Party and led to the Opposing Forces in the Black community that Dr. King wrote about.

The Opposing Forces

Name-calling and complicity with racist by the opposing forces Dr. King named were my motivation for naming and writing this book. The opposing forces inside the Black community and the media are dressed up as social justice warriors and spreading hate. Who they are and what they are hiding is documented in this book.

President Reagan's claim that Black leaders keep Black people aggrieved backs up my personal experience as a victim of racism. Those "aggrieved" African Americans President Reagan mentioned, along with their elected officials and civil rights leaders have helped cover up discrimination, Klan violence, and even racist murder. However, none of this is possible without an excess of participation and help from the civil rights industry, the media, and others on the far Left. This includes organizations like the NAACP, and the ACLU, and media outlets such as MSNBC.

The claims I have made and will continue making throughout this book are against the same groups of people President Reagan named and Dr. Martin Luther King, Jr. warned about in his book *Letter from Birmingham Jail.* Dr. King writes:

"...I stand in the middle of two opposing forces in the Negro community. One is a force of complacency, made up in part of Negroes who, as a result of long years of oppression, are so drained of self respect and a sense of "somebodiness" that they have adjusted to segregation; and in part of a few middle-class Negroes who, because of a degree of academic and economic security and because in some ways they profit by segregation, have become insensitive to the problems of the masses...."

Today, these Opposing Forces are in charge, and busy erasing Black History. The "D.A.A.M." people today see Dr. King as someone who had a dream that might uncover the nightmare the Left created and hid by creating Critical Race Theory.

The African Americans President Reagan and Dr. King identified are alive and well today. They were pushing racism for profit and political power back then, and they are doing the same thing as of this writing with one big exception. Today, they have far more political and economic power. Today, the descendants of slaves are not trying to end bigotry and oppression with that power. They are just picking up where Jim Crow left off. Social justice causes that were once considered racist, oppressive, and worth dying for are now considered almost chic. As I previously stated, even a former First Lady and Princess are now among the oppressed.

Malcolm X also recognized the same "opposing forces" as President Reagan and Dr. King when he stated that institutional racism would not continue for another single day without the complicity of African American leaders. Many believe both Dr. King and Malcolm X were killed by those opposing forces. Regardless, even with history and evidence on my side, it will not be easy proving that opposing forces exist to people who believe they are victims of White Supremacy in perpetuity and money will be coming soon for what slaves went through.

The opposing forces Dr. King spoke of are the ones exploiting and oppressing African Americans, and not the so-called Vast Right Wing Conspirators Hillary Clinton dreamed up. Those opposing forces use cultural conditioning wrapped in the history of racism to drain African Americans of "...self-respect and a sense of "somebodiness...." African Americans are then used by the Left as voting stock. The Left's mission is complete when they have robbed those in the Black community who follow the narrative of their ability to act in the interest of their community or to use reasoning and logic.

Speaking of reasoning, logic, and conditioning, consider two friends of mine who are African American teachers. One is a principal with a Ph.D. Both believed that Lincoln was a Democrat and LBJ was a Republican. My friends were not taught this in school, and neither teach this in their classrooms. Their beliefs about Lincoln and LBJ are based solely on cultural conditioning.

As a tool in the hands of the Opposing Forces, Cultural Conditioning erased years of their learning. Like most African Americans, my friends assume information is true or false based on their politics. They are bringing their way of thinking into the classroom. Can you imagine the effect learning this way has on our children? Not just Black kids but that White kid with the purple hair taking a knee right beside a Black kid standing and saluting the flag.

Thanks to Dr. King and Malcolm X, We the People no longer have to indict an entire race for the sins of the majority. We know, from their mistreatment of Black Conservatives, what these people are capable of. These opposing forces in the Black culture have moved the Black community from legitimate grievances to full-blown mental illness. This illness will be exacerbated because they currently have no opposition.

Another example of cultural conditioning being used as a tool is playing out before our eyes. The Opposing Forces in the Black community spent decades accusing the FBI and CIA of bringing drugs into the Black community, killing Malcolm X and Dr. King. Now that both the FBI and CIA have been caught dirty, Woke African Americans trust them and are now on their side.

The following chapters will introduce many of the Opposing Forces and exemplify their complicity with racists. The revelation came for me in January 1979. Nothing I faced throughout my childhood in the Jim Crow South, or my 60 years of activism comes close to what followed when I filed a discrimination complaint against the North Carolina Department of Corrections over the racism and Klan activity at Moore County Prison unit in Carthage, North Carolina.

Black-on-Black Racism
Bobby Person Jimmie Pratt VS NCDOC
Person VS the Carolina Knights of the KKK

Between 1979 and 1984, I worked at the Moore County Prison in Carthage, North Carolina under a Federal jobs program called the Comprehensive Education Training Act, better known as CETA. During this time, the Governor was James Hunt, a Democrat. Under his administration, statewide racial discrimination was rampant in the state employee hiring and promotional system and its agencies.

From my first day on the job until I was discharged in 1984, working at the Moore unit was a racial nightmare. For perspective, I spent the first 16 years of my life in the Jim Crow South and never experienced that degree of racism. Every day Black officers were humiliated and discriminated against. The humiliation was in addition to being denied promotional opportunities and given appraisals that did not reflect our job performance.

13

I remember the day I first confronted Captain Marion about the racism he was enabling. Present with Captain Marion was Lieutenant Saunders. I told Captain Marion I planned to file a complaint with the NAACP. In response, both Captain Marion and Lieutenant Saunders started laughing. Captain Marion handed me the phone and offered me the number. Offering to dial the number would be prophetic. In other words, Captain Marion action meant that I would not be getting any help from the Black leadership class and he knew it.

The only time the racism ceased a bit was when I was working the third shift. The inmates were asleep, and Captain Marion was gone. However, the Black officers working the day shift faced blatant acts of discrimination in the form of using the "N-word" jokes, harassment, abuse, retaliation, and overt threats from staff and White officers who had joined the Klan. At the Moore County unit, minority inmates faced the same daily degradation, which eventually led to death. More on the deaths later.

Years of this mistreatment and racism at the Moore unit led me to confrontations with supervisory staff members on various occasions. For example, every day except Saturday and Sunday, Captain Marion had a policy of assigning Black officers to the guard tower in the back of the prison or the dormitory where visitors could not see us. Inmates called the back tower the "Black Tower." It was an assignment to humiliate Black officers. However on Sunday, visiting day, White officers were assigned to the "Black Tower" because visitors came to the prison to visit inmates and he did not want us seen. When I arrived at work on this particular Sunday, I decided this was the day to make a stand. I was not having any more of the racism. Sergeant Martindale called me on the intercom and said he was assigning me to the "Front Tower." Understand, except for Saturday and Sunday, the Front Tower was off-limits to Black officers. Instead of going to the Front Tower, I went straight to my car and drove home.

After a week passed, I received a call from the Area Administrator, Johnny Cole. He wanted to know when I was returning to work. I was shocked: I had been assuming I had been fired. I guess they didn't have all their ducks in a row, or they didn't know my plans.

Before I returned to work, Mr. Cole wanted me to meet him at a park in Carthage, near the prison. We agreed that I would return to work at the Moore unit for 30 days and transfer to the Hoke unit. I had no intention of keeping that promise when I made it. Consequently. when the 30 days were up, I refused to go. I cannot explain why conditions were temporarily better. Black officers were allowed to work on the Front Tower during the week and the visiting area on Sundays. It did not last, and soon there was another confrontation.

On this particular weekday, I had been assigned to the Front Tower when the laundry truck came. The White driver was well known for making racial slurs about inmates. I was outside on the tower's ledge with the shotgun while inmates were unloading the laundry truck. I overheard the laundry truck driver say to Sergeant

Martindale, "Is he still causing trouble?" I snapped. I pointed the shotgun and told them to shut up. At this late date, I don't remember what else I said.

In retrospect, I now realize that I was slowly going insane. I say this because, later, I tried to hide one of the pistols assigned to the guard tower. I planned to retrieve the weapon, hide on Captain Marion's route home, and shoot him. Luckily for me, another officer found the pistol, and assumed it had fallen behind the commode.

Before I was employed at the Moore unit, Black officers had never taken the promotional exam. I can remember telling a White officer named Wadsworth, who I was friendly with, that I was going to take the "test" as soon as I was eligible for it. Wadsworth told me that Captain Marion had said, "as long as he's running the prison, he is not promoting any "Jigga Boos."

When we met the two-year requirements, four Black officers at the Moore unit, including me, went to Salemburg and took the promotional examination. However, before we received our test scores, Captain Marion told us we had failed. The next time the exam came around, fellow officer Bobby Person and I retook the exam. Long before I took a stand against Captain Marion, I would go to wherever Bobby was assigned and say to him "are you still with me" and he would always reply with "as long as you tell the truth." Despite being on different sides of the political divide, Our stand against racism and intolerance has made us friends for life.

After the test, Captain Marion called us into his office. He told us we had passed, and they had Sergeant positions for us at the Troy unit in Montgomery County. We said, "No thank you." We told Captain Marion we wanted our promotions at the Moore County unit where we were being denied opportunities. Immediately, Captain Marion said, "then all of you failed."

Each time I tried to appeal to authorities for help, I was rebuffed and conditions got worse. The state's refusal to respond, and civil rights groups refusing to help, made it clear I had no support other than Bobby Person. After two years of this, the only thing left was to turn to God. I can remember one weekend being on the guard towers praying to God not to let me lose my home or my car, or to let my children go hungry. I knew if I filed a complaint against Captain Marion, I would lose my job and more. When my tower duty ended after that prayer, I had no fear. I had power. I walked into Captain Marion's office, took his picture off from the wall, and threw it into the garbage can. I had thrown down the gauntlet at the feet of tyranny. There would be no discrimination today, tomorrow, or ever again, I thought.

Shortly after that incident, I wrote to the Secretary of Correction, James Woodard, about the racism at the prison. Months passed, and there was no investigation. I contacted the Chicago office of PUSH and asked for help. The director of the chapter told me PUSH only helped members and suggested we join. Both Bobby Person and I paid the membership dues and joined. After I received my membership card, I called the PUSH office; the director asked me, "What do you think we can do from out here?" The NAACP, SCLC, ACORN, and the other civil rights groups followed the example set by PUSH.

After the PUSH rejection, I went to bed, as I usually do, with the TV on. I was awakened by a Raleigh News and Observer commercial. I heard the announcer say, "We are the ones to call when you want to fight City Hall," I knew immediately from the ad what I had to do. I wrote to the Raleigh News and Observer about the complaint sent to Secretary Woodard. By the way, this happens to be the newspaper provided to inmates daily.

A week or two later, inmates asked me what had been cut out of the newspaper. When I got off work, I bought a copy of the Raleigh News and Observer. They had reported my complaint and the prison staff had cut it out of the newspaper before giving it to inmates. The News and Observer reported the complaint but never interviewed any of us to this day. That same afternoon, Channel Five news came to the prison after I left work. That, too, foretold more of the same to come. I soon found out the press was conspiring with the North Carolina Department of Correction (NCDOC).

Federal Equal Employment Law requires all employees filing workplace discrimination complaints to first follow the employer's personnel rules and allow employers to investigate first. The NCDOC did not follow their own personnel policy. Instead of investigating, the NCDOC sent out a news release announcing they had completed their investigation and found no discrimination. There was one problem. There had been no investigation. Once the NCDOC had been caught, they decided to do another fake investigation that included statements from Black officers. The findings and recommendations from the fake investigation matched the information cited in the fake news release.

The date on the news release was November 2, 1981. The date of the fake investigation was March 29, 1983. Almost two years had passed since the release of the fake press release. The state spent those two years handing out promotions to Black officers and state employees throughout the state government.

I knew nothing about the fake press release until I ran into a friend who said to me: "I told you they were not going to do anything." He told me the local radio station WEEB had aired the investigation results and found no discrimination. I immediately drove to WEEB Radio and asked to speak to the station's manager. He confirmed what my friend had told me. I told him that I was the plaintiff and assured him the state had not investigated. I remember him being outraged that the DOC had him air a lie. Several days later, the station manager called and invited Bobby and me to refute the press release and tell our story. The station manager gave me a copy of the news release.

When the state finally completed the investigation they were forced to conduct, it was a mockery. The investigator cited actual acts of racism and claimed in his report it was "unprofessional language." For instance, In paragraph 1 of the Recommendations from the investigation, Robert Mathes states that Superintendant Marion called an employee "Nigger." The truth is Superintendant Marion called many Black employees Nigger, but we will stick with what the state admits.

****

Robert Mathes revealed in his investigation that Superintendant Marion had promoted no Black officers and used racial slurs. This is racism under Title VII because the offenses created a hostile work environment. Today White people using such language would be the subject of retribution even if it was said when they were ten years old. Robert Mathes, the African American investigator, ignored his findings and found: "….no discrimination, only unprofessional language…" In his investigation, Mathes did not mention the fact that White officers had handed racist material to inmates. I still have a copy of the racist job application passed out to immates.

Some forty-plus years later, I still cannot understand why Robert Mathes revealed in his report that Captain Marion called us Niggers but found no discrimination. The state, their allies in the media, and civil rights leaders had invested a lot of time and energy into lying and covering up everything. So why admit this? Was it to mock us? I don't know; , but we will stick with what the state admits

After Robert Mathes finished his investigation, he told me I would be fired. He also wrote in his investigation that I had 40 policy violations. The NCDOC fired me, and Captain Marion was issued an "Oral "Warning after calling an Employee a Nigger and not promoting any Black officers, ever. To make matters worse, while watching the United Negro College Telethon, Robert Mathes appeared on the show to donate money to help the same Black people he was crushing.

****

Bobby Person and I disagreed with the investigation and filed a discrimination complaint with the Equal Employment Opportunity Commission (EEOC). We would find out that the EEOC was even more corrupt than the NCDOC and the press. The racism, malfeasance, and corruption at the EEOC are well known. As with all other obstacles placed in our way, the EEOC's investigation of our case was carried out by people who looked like us or another minority.

The first EEOC investigator was White. He called and told me he was ruling against the NCDOC and in my favor. Like most people in the legal and civil rights fields who promised to help, he too disappeared. In other words, I didn't hear from him again. After waiting months for an update on my complaint, I called the EEOC.

Fortunately, not having my file number connected me with an honest person at the EEOC. When the receptionist asked for my file number, I gave her my name because I did not have my case number. After hearing my name only, the receptionist knew of my case file. She immediately told me that I had better find someone to get my case out of the hands of the Administrative Judge who had it. She told me to contact Sam, whose last name I have since forgotten. I contacted him, and he promised me he would make things right. Within a month, I could not get hold of Sam.

However, the secretary's first-hand knowledge of our case from among tens of thousands of cases tells me she knew our case was being mishandled and the knowledge of the misconduct was well known within the EEOC. I would find out later that our complaint had been turned over to the District manager, Robert Amoruso. He accepted the DOC investigation without investigating himself or asking for input from Bobby and me or any officers. However, we were given a "Right to Sue" letter by the EEOC and sue is what we did.

Having a Right to Sue letter meant Bobby and I could sue for discrimination in the Federal Courts. Now we needed a lawyer. Former North Carolina Governor James Holshouser had opened a law office in Southern Pines. I knew he would not help, but I asked anyway. I'm sure it was primarily out of curiosity that he asked me to come in. After I told him my story, he said that being a former governor, he could not in good faith represent me. He told me that I should get a lawyer from out of town. I saw a Raleigh Yellow Pages phone book on his table and asked if I could have it. The Yellow Pages phone book had pages filled with discrimination attorneys. When I arrived home, I closed my eyes and called the lawyer where my finger landed. The law firm was Edelstein, Payne, and Jordon.

Travis Payne was the attorney assigned to our case. He filed a lawsuit alleging that Black officers at the Moore unit were denied promotional opportunities, and the promotional exam was biased. The law firm Edelstein, Payne, and Jordan was well connected to the non-legacy civil rights community. Through them, we were introduced to groups like Southerners for Economic Justice, North Carolinians Against Race And Religious Violence, and Jim Grant from Black Workers for Justice. Almost weekly, Jim Grant would drive over from Raleigh to Bobby's house when the Klan showed up to harass him and his family. Bobby and I would later serve on the board of North Carolinians Against Race And Religious Violence.

The Democrats were playing hardball with the lawsuit. With the media and civil rights leaders in their pockets, the NCDOC felt they did not have to settle. It wasn't until a Republican was elected Governor of North Carolina that settlement talks began. Shortly after his election, Governor Martin appointed Aaron Johnson, a Black man, as Secretary of Corrections, and we settled. I guess Republicans did not have the protection of the press and civil rights groups.

In the settlement, I received $40,000, and I had to agree not to ask for my job back. I also agreed not to work for the state of North

Carolina. I thought it was a bad deal. But having had no extra money for three years, I took it. However, the most baffling part of the settlement was the part concerning Bobby. Although Bobby was a plaintiff with ten years of seniority, the agreement called for Bobby to be the second Black Sergeant at the Moore unit. The first promotion to sergeant went to a Black officer named Jerry Kelly, who had been working at the unit less than two years when Bobby and I had sued the Department of Corrections. Kelly was the only Black officer who had said he saw no discrimination at the prison. By definition, a settlement offering Bobby the second sergeant position when he was the injured party was retaliation and a violation of Title VII.

Typically, a lawsuit about racism and the Klan would be front-page news and a fundraising goldmine for civil rights groups. As you will learn from the information provided here, the media has an economic, social, and ideological agenda when it comes to racism or discrimination in the workplace. Whether printed or broadcasted, news that hurts Democrats and the Left were edited out of the news cycle. On the other hand, news stories that hurt Republicans were reported with extreme bias, much like today. The NAACP and other civil rights groups ignored the racism at the prison and joined in a cover-up that included protecting the Klan.

Neither the civil rights groups nor the press could ignore White officers joining a Klan group with a leader who was already on the Southern Poverty Law Center radar and had connections to the hate group, The Order, an Aryan resistance movement This could only mean one thing. Morris Dees, a co-founder of the Southern

Poverty Law Center, was on the way to help himself, and not us.

Because fellow officer Jerry Mike Lewis harassed and burned a cross at Bobby's house. was a member of the Carolina Knights of the KKK headed by Glenn Miller, the Southern Poverty Law Center (SPLC) filed a lawsuit against the group on behalf of Bobby Person and others in the state of North Carolina. On page 214 of Morris Dees' book *A Lawyer's Journey,* Morris writes: "...We had been looking for the opportunity to go after Miller..." The SPLC taking the case meant the lawsuit would become national and international news. However, Morris Dees taking the case also meant the story about Black officers being denied opportunities at the prison had to be changed for the press to report it. Our story about the lack of equal opportunity for Black officers became an opportunity for the media and the civil rights industry to lie and conspire. The media tagged along with Morris Dees, which meant that what had happened at the Moore County Prison would stay at the prison which will be explained later.

****

To take attention off the prison, the press framed the racism at the prison as one man having been given an opportunity that the Klan didn't like. Once the racial narrative was changed, the news media was ready to report their version. Now that the fix was in, there would be many press conferences and guest appearances on local and national talk shows. Bobby and I would learn the hard way. None of the publicity was about us or what had happened to Black officers at the Moore County Prison.

The appearance of the Klan had achieved what they had been called in to do. They were wagging the dog to keep the public from discovering what was happening at the prison. It worked because it took all the attention off the Moore prison unit. I believe to this day that people in the civil rights community ordered the appearance of the Klan.

I say the Klan was ordered to do this because the racism at the Moore County Prison did not completely fit the racial narrative of White on Black or White male-only racism. The people who ordered the Klan to show up at the prison are the ones Dr. King described as: ..." *a few middle-class Negroes who, because of a degree of academic and economic security and because in some ways they profit by segregation, have become insensitive to the problems of the masses....*"

The Opposing Forces Dr. King warned about were in charge. Harold Webb, the State Personnel Director, Juanita Baker, the Prison Personnel Director, and Robert Mathes, the Equal Employment Officer, were all African Americans, and Democrats These three African Americans were in charge of policing discrimination and making policy for the entire NC State and prison employee system. Their job was to enforce Equal Opportunity Laws and investigate discrimination charges, among other duties. They were tokens; they were trailblazers, as the "First Blacks in those positions for the Democrat Party. They were the reason everything about the Moore County Prison had to be covered up.

The fake news release, I mentioned earlier, was the beginning of the campaign by the State of North Carolina to cover for these three African Americans. The press and the civil rights community did not want the public to know that African Americans were in charge of a prison and state employee system immersed in racism. No way was the press going to expose Juanita Baker, the wife of Wake County's first Black Sheriff, and Harold Webb, a Tuskegee Airman, as the faces of White Supremacy. The cover-up was so widespread, it would be easier for me to leave out all the news organizations, civil rights leaders, and politicians who participated in this cover-up than to name those who did not.

Racism at the Moore unit had put the press and the civil rights community in a Catch-22 position. To free themselves, all the racism at the prison became a story about one officer and the KKK. They changed all the racism at the Moore County Prison Unit to fit the "White Male Only" or White on Black racial narrative.

On the SPLC website is a column titled SPLC, Landmark Cases: Bobby Person. This article is the script the press followed. The report claimed that Bobby Person applied for a position and the Klan came after him. When the SPLC published that article, they knew that eight of the nine Black officers had said they were the victims of racial discrimination. In addition, the same information came from the state's investigation. Robert Mathes writes in his investigation report that all but one Black officer complained of racism. There is no disputing the complaint, and the lawsuits were both filed by two men, Bobby Person, and me against the prison. So how can it be about one man and the Klan? From the moment the press found out African

Americans were in charge, the MSM (Mainstream Media) reported nothing about what had really happened at the prison.

Black officers were not the only people abused in the North Carolina Prison system. Inmates of color were facing the same racism Black officers faced. The unchecked abuse finally ended in deaths at the Moore and Hoke prisons. I filed a complaint with the Justice Department on behalf of Robert Kennedy and other inmates. Robert Kennedy was one of the two inmates who died after the staff denied both Kenneth Royall and him medical treatment at the Moore and Hoke County units.

Officers and inmates sent me a petition asking if I would try to find help for inmate Robert Kennedy at the Moore unit. For weeks, inmate Robert Kennedy was so weak that he could not walk. After he collapsed, prison staff chained him up and drove him to the hospital. He died on February 8, which happens to be my birthday. The cause of death was undiagnosed diabetes. I remember the officers who took Kennedy to the hospital telling me that the doctor who treated Kennedy scolded the prison nurse for being neglectful. I contacted the local NAACP, the ACLU and wrote to legislators, the NCDOC, and the news media. They offered no help.

****

Around the same time inmate Robert Kennedy was dying, Kenneth Royall was serving his sentence at the Hoke County Unit. Kenneth Royall was an alcoholic, who was in prison for not taking his TB medicine, a crime in North Carolina. In both cases, inmates and officers alike reported that Royall too was denied medical treatment by the prison medical staff. The press reported that State Representative James Craven was investigating both inmates' deaths. Like everything else concerning this prison system run by African Americans, the investigation into both inmates' deaths was squashed too. While the press was burying the deaths of these inmates, Bobby and I were entering a full-blown war with the Carolina Knights of the Ku Klux Klan.

Before the NCDOC fired me, racist Klan literature started appearing at the prison. Drive-by shootings and harassment against Black officers by the Klan soon followed the literature. The shootings only happened when Black officers were working on Tower #3 in the back of the prison next to the highway. Clearly, someone inside the prison was telling the Klan when Black officers were on Tower #3. In the early morning, while still dark, someone in a vehicle would drive down Highway 15501 and shoot at the tower. The Moore County Sheriff Department said Black officers were making it up. We knew they were co-workers from their behavior, and we knew their names.

The Dual system of Discrimination

In a way, I sympathized with White officers. I understood the effect that Black officers taking the promotional exam under Affirmative Action had on White officers. It is important to understand that there was a dual system of bigotry in hiring and promotion. For Black officers, it was racial bigotry, and for White officers, it was nepotism. Both forms of discrimination affected both Black and White officers regarding promotions. If they were not related to any seniors, White officers at the Moore unit, they were also passed over for promotions. White officers and Black officers alike were being denied advancement.

In a bizarre kind of reverse or reserved discrimination, there were White officers in the NCDOC who had passed the promotional exam long before the first Black officers were hired to work at the prison. However, to make White officers feel superior, they were given assignments and special duties that Black officers were not allowed to do. The discrimination against White officers also meant that discrimination against Black officers was more profound and often committed by the same White officers who faced discrimination. Unlike White officers, who had no legal recourse, Black officers did. It was called Title VII. Bobby Person and I used it to file our complaint with the EEOC.

Black officers taking the exam also gave Superintendent Marion the excuse he needed to drive a wedge between White and Black officers. He told White officers that word had come down from Raleigh to promote Black officers over White officers. In response, a couple of White officers joined the Carolina Knights of the KKK and began harassing Black officers at their homes and prisons.

****

Given all the racism and discrimination, the Klan showing up seems timed as they were in the "nick of time." The Klan took all the attention off the prison. It gave the media an acceptable reason to ignore and edit out of the news cycle the racism and Klan activity going on in and around the prison.

Bobby Person and I considered our fellow officer Jerry Mike Lewis and his friend Gregory Short good friends until they burned a cross at Bobby's house. Before Lewis joined the Klan, he ate lunch with Black officers, dressed Black, tried to talk Black, and always gave the Black handshake. After work, Lewis, I, and other White officers would get a bottle of whiskey, sit in the car and drink with no cups.

The relationship between Bobby and Klansman Gregory Short was even closer. When Gregory Short was a child, his father would get drunk and kick Gregory and his mother out of their home. Although this was during the Jim Crow era, Gregory Short and his mother had lived with Bobby and his family. Bobby's father was still taking Gregory Short back and forth to work as an adult. That is until he and Mike Lewis burned a cross at Bobby's house and scratched KKK into the side of Bobby's father's pickup.

On one occasion, Jerry Mike Lewis, Gregory Short, and Short's wife Joan came to Bobby's house armed and dressed in full Klan regalia. They scratched KKK into the side of Bobby's father's truck, and vandalized Bobby's family church before returning later in the month. When they returned, Bobby was at home with a furniture salesman, who became terrified. Bobby grabbed his rifle and got behind a tree. Lewis demanded Bobby come from behind the tree so he could "whoop his ass. After the confrontation, Bobby swore out a warrant on Lewis and the Shorts. They, in return, had arrest warrants issued for Bobby. A Moore County Judge threw out both cases. Lewis told us later that the local NAACP had paid the Klan to vandalize the church, and that is why he and other Klansmen were laughing at us in court. By the way, I'm told Short's wife is now married to a Black man.

Lewis, Short, and other Klansmen were harassing Bobby and his family almost weekly. The harassment was so regular, I virtually lived at Bobby's house. Bobby and I were joined later by an activist from Black Workers for Justice named Jim Grant. Two brothers, Hilton and Wilton Dunlap, also correctional officers, joined us. Bobby, Jim, and I were Vietnam Veterans., Hilton and his brother Wilton were Army Veterans. When the Klan showed up at Bobby's house, we would show up armed and ready to do battle.

On another occasion, Mike Lewis came to Bobby's house while I was there. I grabbed my rifle and pistol and went out to the road. Lewis drove up to the church at the end of the street, turned around, and drove slowly back towards Bobby's house. I was standing in the road, locked, and loaded. Lewis stopped and asked me to drink a beer like old times. I told him "no" because I planned to shoot him. Lewis said he just wanted to apologize to Bobby for all he had done. Lewis also said he had Sergeant Sudderth with him in the car, but Sudderth jumped out when he saw where Lewis was headed. Lewis then asked me if he could pull into the yard to get off the road. I told him he could. Bobby, who was in the house on the phone with the Moore County Sheriff Department, came running out yelling for Lewis not to pull into the yard. Bobby thought I wanted Lewis to pull into the yard so I would have an excuse to shoot him. That was my excuse to beat him with the butt of my rifle.

****

After months of harassment by the Klan, Bobby and I decided to drive by Lewis's house that served as a Klan den. We loaded up our weapons and drove slowly by Lewis's home. Lewis and other Klansmen were in the yard. They pointed at us and started walking towards the road, yelling obscenities but thought better of it. They probably thought we were setting up an ambush, and we were.

At this time, the Carolina Knights of the KKK leader was Glenn Miller. As the head of the largest Klan group in America, Miller, as I previously mentioned, was on the Southern Poverty Law Center's radar. Morris Dees, using a Federal statute reserved for the Mafia and terrorists, sued the Carolina Knights of the KKK, Mike Lewis, Gregory Short, and Short's wife Joan for one million dollars.

The lawsuits against the Carolina Knights of the KKK and the NCDOC bought down the largest Klan group in America. This followed Bobby and my lawsuit that gave the first promotions for African Americans at the prison and through the state employee system. In exchange for dropping the million-dollar lawsuit, Miller agreed to an order banning his Klan group from marching in any Black community, and from harassing or intimidating Black citizens in the state of North Carolina.

In an attempt to invalidate the agreement, Miller changed the name of his group to the White Patriot Party and continued harassing Black people. He wrongly assumed the name change voided the Consent Decree. For violating the court order, Miller and his Klan were taken back to court and found guilty of violating the Consent Decree. Rather than go to prison, Miller went underground and promised to start a race war. When the FBI raided the place where Miller was hiding, Miller surrendered and decided to snitch and rat out Klan members across the nation. After serving a couple of years of his Federal sentence, Miller entered the Witness Protection Program and moved to Kansas under the name of Frazier Glenn Cross. Miller later murdered three White people he thought were Jews and was sentenced to death. He died on Death Row before Kansas could execute him.

Even after the death of Glenn Miller, the press continued the cover-up. When reporting on his death, the press erased everything Miller had done to Black people in North Carolina, Moore County, and elsewhere. Most Americans do not know that Glenn Miller also participated in the Greensboro Massacre, in which five Communist Workers Party members were murdered. Miller was not charged for any of these murders. White Patriot Party members were also implicated in the execution-style murder of three people, believed to be gay, in a Shelby adult gay bookstore in 1987.

So, tell me. How is it that Glenn Miller, the most notorious Klan leader, and hatemonger of the Twentieth Century, dies in May of 2021, and the Left is completely silent? I could not find anything about his death on the Southern Poverty Law Center website. Miller dies, and Bobby Person, the man responsible for his downfall, is not interviewed or asked how he feels about the death. With Miller's death, the headlines changed again to put the final nail in the coffin of the Moore County Prison. This time they changed so that history would record Glen Miller's life as the murderer of three innocent White people he thought were Jews.

While the press was burying our piece of civil rights history, the people who consistently complain that Black History is not taught in schools are now faced with a civil rights history they don't want to be told or taught. Keeping hate alive is why the Left created Critical Race Theory and BLM to push it.

All across the nation and on social media, the Left is pushing Critical Race Theory to ensure that Black History is scrubbed clean of the history they are trying to cover up. In its place, they want a race theory taught that is part of their indoctrination campaign. According to the Left, people of color in the wrong social class or on the wrong side of the political and racial divide do not deserve a history. Although Bobby was on the right side of the political divide, he and I filing a civil rights complaint against a state with a Democrat governor had to kept from recorded history.

Complicity Racism Theory: (CRT)

White Liberals or progressives have the patience of Job from the Bible. Social issues like those regarding transgender, immigration, abortion, and racism are designed to create permanent victim classes of whiners. The entire base of the Democrat Party is made up of people with a bone to pick. The Left nurtures these groups of mostly mentally ill people to political maturity. When the time is right, as in the election of 2020, the Left turns grievances into votes.

The Left exploits rather than offers solutions for issues like racism, gender dysphoria, and abortion. For these votes, Democrats spend decades keeping their base feeling picked on. In the end, the Left knows the victims they create will support them no matter what. These victims of the Left have been "…had, ran amuck and led astray," to quote Malcolm X. They are completely loyal to an ideology that harvests their vote even though the only thing they accomplished was adding new letters to the LGBTQ+ acronym, killing women's sports, and aborting 40 percent of the Black population.

Corporations, politicians, the Klan, and anyone who exploits hatred and racism follow the model of the Left. When politicians and Corporations need to appear "woke," they will use equity and employ the services of prominent African Americans. By putting prominent African Americans in strategic positions of influence and power, the Left and Corporate America can use racism to hold at bay the Constitution, label Americans they disagree with, and avoid scrutiny. Prominent African Americans who control people for a living know that African Americans are not afraid of White people putting Black people back in chains. African Americans are afraid of other African Americans. They know White people will never do to them what they will do to each other.

If you are Black and President Biden's illegal mandates feel like déjà vu, you are reliving your past. Long before COVID-19, the Black community was used to perfect all those mandates and get the desired outcome. The practice of getting large groups of people to stay silent while being used, misled, and lied to was created using the Black community as a Pavlovian laboratory. Maybe I should just say it was culturally appropriate. That way, going along with things to get along can be blamed on White people later on.

The Left and the Democrats' tools to force compliance, win elections, divide the nation, and control the behavior of entire groups of people all came out of the Black experience. No other study explains that experience more thoroughly than the Moynihan Report. This report predicted the decline of the Black family we see today. The Left built their scheme on the good intention of that report. The

Left knew from the Moynihan Report you needed to destroy the Black family first or as you go along.

The charges I'm making may seem repetitive and even a bit harsh because the intent is to enlighten. Unless Woke African Americans' involvement in the oppression and exploitation of Black people is reported and acted on, The Black family will be destroyed and the majority will continue to live on the Democrat Plantation as Voting Stock. Conservatives of all races can no longer afford to leave their defense to a class of Republicans with their finger consistently measuring the political winds. Only a grassroots Conservative movement led by the people falsely accused of being racist and Uncle Toms will put an end to the Left's agenda.

Unless Conservatives and Republicans who defend the truth start to push back, names and acronyms like BLM, ANTIFA, NAACP, MSM, KKK, Planned Parenthood, Gender Diaspora, Systemic Racism, and Equity will continue to be a source of blackmail, oppression, terror, and winning elections The evidence in this book proves that the people accusing others of being racist have a far worse history of being racist than any Conservative or Republican. Conservatives and Republicans should never forget that Democrats perfected the use of hate to extract votes, divide people, and get their victims to fight their political wars.

Since COVID started, White Americans have been experiencing what life for Black people was like under Jim Crow. Only this time African American Democrats are the military wing of the party instead of the Ku Klux Klan. Americans who are not

Democrats are being jailed, medicine is rationed according to color and all must pass a narrative test. This system of bigotry shows no mercy or compassion for Conservatives.

I have lived and documented the collaboration between the press, the Democrat Party, and African American leaders for more than 40 years. In that period, I kept documents that prove the NAACP, PUSH/Rainbow, the Southern Poverty Law Center, the NY Times, the Charlotte Observer, the Washington Post, the Raleigh News and Observer, WTVD, WFMY, ABC, CBS, NBC, A&E, the EEOC, the Congressional Black Caucus, Professor Irving Joyner, and many others openly covered up racism, racist murder, and Klan violence against people of color. I named them without fear of libel or defamation suits because I lived the charges I'm making. However, it will take this divided America to tell the whole truth about racism. When we the people know the truth, all of America will then know why we cannot seem to get a handle on racism.

****

My personal experience is not the only source for evidence that complicity racism exists. Black issues being deliberately ignored by Woke African American elected officials and civil rights leaders can googled. The proof can be seen in a YouTube video of a town hall meeting sponsored by the Congressional Black Caucus. In that meeting, Black voters wanted action from Obama. They demanded that Maxine Waters confront Obama over unemployment and other issues. Waters responded by saying the Congressional Black Caucus wanted to have a conversation with the President but was hesitating because African American voters would "come after them" if the CBC confronted Obama. The video can be viewed using this link.

https://www.youtube.com/watch?v=3tVf6fwMFQ4)

Al Sharpton used the same dodge on Black issues when Lesley Stahl of 60 Minutes asked him about confronting Obama. Al Sharpton responded by saying:" … He never promised to go with a Black agenda, Duh!"

https://youtu.be/UHoMXLSjlDo

Maxine Waters and Al Sharpton can get away with ignoring the wishes of Black people. On the other hand, Black Americans have been killed for offering solutions and asking the wrong party for help. That is what happened to Bernell Trammell when he attempted to get African Americans to demand something for their vote. As in this case, the Left tries to silence real victims of discrimination because these victims are the keepers of the truth. Because of their experience, they know where all the bodies are buried. Black victims of racism also know from experience one cannot buy help or get help to fight racism from any of the groups supposedly fighting racism. They also know it's hazardous to your health to ask. This is why I tell victims of racism it is better to put up with the racism than trust the process.

The lawsuits filed by Bobby Person and me against the NCDOC and Bobby against the Carolina Knights of the Ku Klux Klan did not advance the cause of social justice. However, The lawsuits did create a new kind of hate group as well as a new kind of gullibility.

Rather than offer support, our community, the civil rights industry, and the African American Ruling Class accused Bobby and me of stirring up trouble and getting out of our place. It did not matter that the landmark lawsuits Bobby and I won against the Klan and the NCDOC bought down the largest Klan group in America and led to the first promotions for Black officers in the North Carolina State Employee System. To this day, our community will not bring it up. All of this happened to Bobby and me because African Americans were in charge of a state and prison personnel system steeped in racism, and we aired the dirty laundry.

Woke African Americans always find an excuse to hate other Black people for things being done by Democrats. When Democrats are caught plucking pages from their racial history, the Biden Administration and other White Democrats can depend on the Congressional Black Caucus and African American Democrat voters to rescue them. When a "D" for Democrat is in front of your name, it's White Privilege.

African American voters came to the aid of Southern racists like Senators Byrd and Richard Long, Governors Wallace, Ralph Northam, and other White supremacists. These same people turned right around and accused Black Conservatives who never supported segregation or owned slaves, of being White Supremacists. According to Woke African Americans, Winsome Sears, the Lieutenant Governor of Virginia, is a White Supremacist and not the first Black to hold that seat.

Remember the Haitians at the border in 2021? Rather than blame President Biden for what they viewed as the racist treatment of Haitians, Woke African American Democrats blamed the agency, the horses, and the Border Agents riding the horses. Other examples would be President Biden's refusal to shake Vice President Harris's hand or sit next to her at Senator Dole's funeral. And of course, there was the leaked audio of Biden telling Al Sharpton and others that African Americans had better "learn to get along" with Hispanics. In each case, President Biden got a pass while Larry Elders and others Conservative Blacks became the face of White Supremacists.

Having spent the first 16 years of my life in the Jim Crow

42

South, I have seen legal racism. However, the most obstacles and hate I faced while living with and opposing racism did not come from the people committing the racist acts. It came from White Liberal racists and African Americans.

After leaving North Carolina, I moved to liberal Alexandria, Virginia outside of DC. The same racial collaboration followed me there. I found work at Unisourse, which later became Monumental Paper Company. When the company moved from Alexandria to PG County, Maryland and then to Baltimore in Maryland, I and others followed the company and made the long commute even though it meant taking a pay cut. Sometime later, a White co-worker told me they had been given a raise rather than a pay cut. I complained to the company about cutting the salaries of Black workers and not the wages of White workers.

A few days after I made the complaint, my supervisor, Bill Carlos, called me into his office. Present with Bill was Torrance Pack, an African American who would later be a witness against me in court. In our discussion, I told Bill I had gone to the doctor because of stress caused by bigotry. Bill suggested that I quit if I was so stressed. I responded by saying, "I went to the doctor because I don't want to become one of "those postal workers" who went on killing sprees in the 80s.The following morning while I was working, two Baltimore City police officers came in. Bill Carlos and Torrance Pack claimed I had threatened the safety of employees with my reference to postal workers. I was fired and escorted off the property.

After my firing, I filed a complaint with the EEOC. Like my

other cases with the NCDOC, the African American investigator at the EEOC found no discrimination. The discrimination I faced at Monumental Paper was so egregious, the judge asked his former law firm to represent me for free. In each of my cases against the NCDOC and Monumental Paper Company, both NC and VA state unemployment agencies ruled in my favor, but the EEOC never did.

****

After settling the lawsuit with Monumental Paper Company, I found another job with Walmer Enterprise in Alexandria, Virginia. There, I ran into more discrimination. By this time, I had to take any job I could find. Walmer Enterprise did not pay minority workers overtime according to law. For example, they did not give minorities time and a half for overtime work. Instead, employees were given their hourly wage plus $1 more for each overtime hour. For easy math, if an employee worked 10 hours overtime at an hourly wage of $10, at "time and a half," that would equal an hourly rate of $15, totaling $150. Instead, Walmer paid its minority employees $11 for an overtime hour rather than $15. Minority employees were paid all overtime in a personal check with no tax taken out. Again, Walmer got away with this because most of their hourly employees were immigrants and were afraid to complain. So they complained to me.

I filed a complaint with the EEOC. Again the state unemployment office supported me, and the EEOC found no discrimination. I kept all the documents to back up my claim. However, when we went to court, Judge Leona Brinkema ordered me to pay Walmer $17,000. Walmer filed a garnishment. But for a reason I do not know, they decided not to make me pay them.

Around this time, I read an article in the Afro newspaper about Shirley Ann Stewart. Shirley was the first female electrician hired by the Department of the Treasury in Washington, DC. When they fired Shirley, she filed a complaint with the EEOC and hired an African American law school dropout named Simon Banks. Banks owned a company called Job Protectors Inc. Banks convinced Shirley and many others to hire him to represent them before the EEOC. After taking their cases, Banks would miss filing deadlines, causing their claims to be dismissed. Because he was Black, no help was coming from the press and civil rights industry. So Shirley and I began protesting at his office, and soon Shirley and I got some help from the Bar association in DC. Mr. Banks ended up in jail.

Before going to jail, Banks was allowed to sue his victims, including Shirley and me, while under indictment. He won some cases against his victims simply because they thought being sued by Banks was too ridiculous to defend and did not show up in court.

I mentioned DC, Fairfax County, PG County, and Baltimore, Maryland because these are some of the most liberal places in America. African Americans ran all but Fairfax County and they were complicit with others in denying victims of discrimination and other civil rights crimes justice. Although I received help from the judge, who was White, trying to get help or justice from the Human Rights Office and legislatures in Counties and cities run by Woke African Americans and Progressives only yielded complicity and heartache.

Mark 6:4: Unwelcome and Unwanted

For opposing racism at the Moore County Prison, Bobby Person and I were as unwelcome as Jesus was when he returned to the place he was born. Bobby was the lead plaintiff in a Class-Action lawsuit against the White Patriot Party. His victory prohibited the Klan from marching in any Black community, and from harassing or intimidating any Black person in the state of North Carolina. The lawsuit filed by Bobby bought down the largest and most dangerous Klan group in America. He and I accomplished this, and to this day, friends and relatives never cite us as race victims or victors when they are condemning racism or honoring victims of racism.

Morris Dees described the significance of this victory over the White Patriot Party by comparing the hate group with another hate group, the United Klan of America. Morris wrote in his book: *"...The UKA was not... in the 1980s, in the same league as the White Patriot Party. Tiger Knowles and Henry Hays used tree limbs and a rope, not rockets and Claymore Mines...."* In other words, The White Patriot Party had military LAW rockets, Claymore Mines, and active-duty soldiers from Fort Bragg in their ranks. The Lawsuits against the Carolina Knights of the KKK/White Patriot Party and the Moore County Prison are now part of North Carolina law and the Library of Congress. However, we will never have a spot in the African American Museum or as much as an asterisk in February on Black History Month.

Instead of "atta boys," Bobby Person and I were as unwanted in our community as Claudette Colvin and the Women before Rosa Parks, after they made their historical contributions. We were as unwelcome by civil rights groups as we were upon returning from Vietnam. Unlike Claudette Colvin, Rosa, in our struggle, was among the oppressors and not the oppressed. As our fight pushed forward, we remained unwelcome in our race. Unfortunately for us, fighting to connect racism and the Klan to the Moore County Prison and being accepted for it became a civil rights struggle of its own.

****

Well before Big Tech began censoring news and speech, the MSM had perfected it. The Black press was even more unwelcoming. The first draft of our Black history, as reported by the media, was corrupted and barely mentioned in the Black media. By denying Bobby and me justice, all these powerful organizations and people succeeded in doing was"raping history."

The small article below is from Jet Magazine. It is a damning indictment summarizing the Black press animus against us. Except for a local Black public affairs program named *Reflections*, this one-column article from Jet Magazine represents the total coverage I know of in the Black press.

Black Charges Klan With Arms Training

A Black prison guard in Moore County, N.C. recently filed a $1million civil suit charging that a Ku Klux Klan group operates a paramilitary army with some 300 members in the state.

Bobby L. Person charged in the suit filed in Federal District Court in Raleigh that members of the Carolina Knights of the Ku Klux Klan had harassed him and his family.

In the Jet article, the magazine does not see Bobby as a person or human but a color. The magazine did not bother with a title or his name. He is just Black, according to the headline. The same is true of family members, friends, and neighbors who continue where Jet Magazine left off.

The Black public affairs TV show Reflection is not without its controversy. The program's collusion is documented in Mabs Segrest's book *Memoir of a Race Traitor*. By the time this show came along, I had decided to stop participating in media events. I stopped talking to the press because they would not report what was going on at the prison nor allow us to criticize the African Americans who either were protecting the Klan or the Klan was protecting. My boycott of the press changed while visiting my daughter in Connecticut. The show's host, Cathy Stowe, called me and reassured me the show would not edit out what we had to say about the prison. Several days after recording the show, I gathered my family in front of the TV to watch the program. The station announced that the show Bobby and I were to appear on had been canceled and they offered no reason. Mabs wrote the following about it in her book

> The resistance to our message when a local television station postponed for two months a Black public affairs program that featured Reverend Lee, Jimmy Pratt, and Bobby Person. It took another petition drive and letters to the Federal Communications Commission to have them air the program.

In the excerpt above from the book, Mabs states that the station canceled the show. However, I found out differently when Leah Wise, head of Southerners for Economic Justice, and I spoke at the Congressional Black Caucus hearing on Klan violence at the NAACP Convention in Charlotte. At that meeting, Leah said the person who filed the complaint was William Becton, the station's Minority Advisory Board President. He filed the complaint stating that I was trying to incite a riot when I said, "we have guns too." After filing a complaint with the FCC, WTVD aired the program with one caveat. Klan leader Glenn Miller was given a half-hour interview with no commercial breaks before they aired the program featuring Bobby and me.

Glenn Miller, the Carolina Knights of the KKK leader, was too valuable to sacrifice by telling what went on at the prison. He was a headline, fundraising, and rating magnet for the Left and the press. Anything Connecting Miller to the Moore County Prison was edited out or avoided, whether at a press conference, radio program, or talk shows. This practice included our appearance on the nationally syndicated talk show *Geraldo*.

Before Bobby and I went to New York, we were told by the producer our segment would be about the lawsuit against the Klan and the racism at the prison. The producer also told us the taping would take place the day after we arrived, and it would just be Bobby and me. I knew something was up when that changed, and we were driven from the airport straight to the set.

Rather than being on a show about our victory over the Klan and the NCDOC, Bobby and I were now appearing with others who, I think, were White and Gay in a segment called "Victims of Klan Violence." I was livid. Bobby and I had almost single-handedly brought down the biggest Klan group in America, and we had to be victims. I did not want to be a victim. Being called a victim puts me in the same mindset as African American Democrats who sees racism everywhere. I felt that I was being turned into a liberal African American who believe the political parties switch because they don't have enough conviction to say they fought and changed the Democrat Party.

No sir, I wanted my victory. Knowing from experience how the media blocked everything about the Moore County Unit, I thought long and hard about how and what I could say and get away with it. After all, I did not want the show to be canceled over something I said. In a roundabout way, I did manage a swipe at civil rights groups. I managed to say that we had received no community or civil rights support.

Our appearance on *Geraldo* exposed the tangled web of deceit Glenn Miller's Klan group posed for the press and civil rights leaders. The media and civil rights groups hiding their agenda inside our social justice struggle was like Churchill's description of Russia. Trying to figure things at times was "a riddle, wrapped in a mystery, inside an enigma." At the same time that they were reporting on and supporting our cause, the press and the entire liberal establishment were corrupting civil rights history to keep it separate from the truth.

Upon returning from our appearance on *Geraldo*, Bobby and I were confronted immediately by two North Carolina SBI agents in the airport's lobby. They took us into a room and questioned us about where we had been. I thought at the time it was because our flying to New York and back overnight fit the profile of drug dealers. We showed the agents our documents from the show plus our prison IDs. We allowed them to search our bags, and we left. I thought that was the end of it. After we were on the highway, the same two SBI agents pulled us over. This time we had our weapons on full display. I forget what they claimed the reason was for pulling us over. However, they did wish us a safe trip home.

After the incident with the SBI agents, the FBI told Bobby and me we were on a Klan hit list. They advised us not to take the same routes going home and to stay vigilant at all times. As for me, I viewed civil rights organizations as more dangerous to my freedom than the Klan

Sometimes, in the race exploitation business, you get hoisted on your own petard or captured by the game. Morris Dees, in his book, *A Season for Justice*, accuses Wake County's Sheriff John Baker, an African American of refusing to protect him and his team in the county courthouse. Because of a conflict of interest, Morris refuses to name the Wake County Sheriff. Morris writes:

> The elevator door opened. We followed our bodyguards out. The hallway was crawling with soldiers in army fatigues and combat boots, Glenn Miller's elite. Terry and his crew formed a wedge and led us through some twenty Klansmen. Most snarled obscenities, some photographed us.
>
> Once we were safe in the conference room, Terry phoned the county sheriff and requested protection. The sheriff, a black man who we assumed would be sympathetic, said he couldn't help us. The death of the Communist organizers in Greensboro and subsequent acquittal of the neo-Nazis and Klansmen accused of murder had made most state

> lawmen suspicious of both
> extremes and wary of
> involvement. The sheriff
> apparently associated us
> with the Communists.

As you can see in the excerpt from Morris's book, he did a little selective editing when it came to outing the first Black Sheriff of Wake County, North Carolina. Rather than name him, Morris described him. I am sure people know or could easily find out that the county sheriff was in charge of the county courthouse's security. Also, it is not hard to find out that the Director of the NCDOC was Sheriff John Baker's wife. Conflict of interest was why the Black sheriff refused to help Morris, and not that they were "extremists," as Morris claimed.

There was, however, a more compelling reason for the selective editing. Neither Morris nor the press would tell the public that Juanita Baker, Director of the North Carolina Department of Correction, was not only African American, but she was also Sheriff Bakers' wife. Yes, the wife of the first Black sheriff was being sued for racism against Black correctional officers. In the end, the lies and deceit Morris was committing in the name of social justice came home to claim him. In a 2019 article about Morris's firing, the LA Times wrote:

> ...employees sent correspondence to management demanding reforms, expressing concerns about the resignation last week of a highly respected black attorney at the organization and criticizing the organization's work culture. A letter signed by about two dozen employees — and sent to management

and the board of directors before news broke of Dees' firing — said they were concerned that internal "allegations of mistreatment, sexual harassment, gender discrimination, and racism threaten the moral authority of this organization and our integrity along with it."

Around 1988, the news media practice of silencing Bobby and I followed us to Hollywood. NBC was producing and distributing a movie based on the life of Bobby's lawyer and co-founder of the Southern Poverty Law Center, Morris Dees. The movie's name was *In the Line of Fire* and it aired in 1991. The writers for the movie put Bobby and me up in a downtown Raleigh hotel to interview us for our characters in the movie. When the writer finished, he told us we had a better story than Morris Dees. He then asked if he could represent us and "shop" our story. As usual, the writer, like many others who started out helping us, soon stopped all communication with us. However, I read some of the reviews of the movie online. Many of those offering criticism wrote that something was missing from the movie. Indeed, something was missing from the movie: us!

In Morris's book, *A Season for Justice*, he writes that our case against the Moore County Prison was the most important case he ever tried. Somehow, the most important case of his life was not in the movie or edited out of the movie. I was not shocked, because civil rights heroes are never poor or working class. I wrote to Morris in 2015 asking him why Bobby and I were not in his movie. Morris responded by writing back that I did not deserve an answer.

The next media exclusion and cover-up came from the A&E documentary, *Hate on Trial: The Klan in America*. Bobby and I heard nothing about the making of this documentary. Once again, the most important case he ever tried was missing. The documentary was based on Morris Dees and his fight against the Klan. The documentary opened with the late Beulah Mae Donald family. Mrs. Donald was the mother of lynching victim Michael Donald. It ended with the Carolina Knights of the KKK/White Patriot Party, Miller's group.

The most significant segment of the documentary was about Glenn Miller, leader of the Carolina Knights of the KKK. This segment begins with the three murders Miller was sent to Death Row for. Fifteen minutes into the documentary, it became the Glenn Miller Show. The only time the broadcast mentioned Bobby Person was to cite the lawsuit that brought down Miller and his organization. The Donald and the Corporon families were interviewed for the documentary. Bobby, whose case brought Miller to Kansas into the Witness Protection Program, was not invited. After the trial ended, Miller was sentenced to death. Only one news organization contacted Bobby Person, the man who started it all.

I wrote to Mrs. Mindy Corporon, whose father and son were murdered by Miller on his killing spree. I wanted her to know the awful game the media, the SPLC, and civil rights leaders had played that led to the murders of her loved one. She sent me her email address, and I responded to her. She never wrote back.

For those murders, Glenn Miller received the death penalty. Upon his sentencing, the press released information about Miller's sexual escapade they had been suppressing for almost forty years. After those three murders, since they had no more use for him, the press reported that Glenn Miller was bisexual, even gay. All of us knew at the time, the police had caught Miller, the Grand Dragon "in the act," with a cross-dressing Black male prostitute. Although nude, Miller said he had been in the back seat with the Black male prostitute to "beat" him up. Somehow, it all just went away.

The 2014 article below described the incident the press should have reported before Miller killed anyone.

> Frazier Glenn Miller, the former Ku Klux Klan "grand dragon" and proud anti-Semite accused of killing three people outside Kansas Jewish centers earlier this month, was not always so strict about his discrimination, at least in private. Before becoming an FBI informant, Miller, who had founded North Carolina's White Patriot Party, was caught in a compromising position — in the backseat of a car — with a black man, doing things a federal prosecutor is not comfortable saying out loud.
> Notorious KKK Leader Frazier Glenn Miller Was Once Caught Doing 'Rather Salacious' Things With a Black Male Prostitute (nymag.com)

Had they outed Miller, I'm sure three innocent people would not have lost their lives. I would like to think a Klansman being caught with a Black male prostitute would have been grounds for immediate ejection from the Klan if not death.

Looking back on Miller's soliciting charge. I had a strange encounter with him during the Federal trial in Raleigh for violating the Consent Decree. When I took a bathroom break, Miller held the door for me. After I entered, Miller followed me to the urinals. He told me that we could not beat the Klan and should give up trying. Looking back on the Grand Dragon holding the door for me, I no longer see it as chivalry.

Shortly before Miller murdered Dr. William L. Corporon, his 14-year-old grandson, Reat Underwood, and Terri LaManno, I called him. I wanted to know why he targeted Black officers at the Moore County Prison and who was behind it. Miller told me he did not authorize any of Mike Lewis's violence. He called Lewis a clown and said other Klansmen in his group had to be watched like babies, or they would kill each other. Before Miller ended the call, he said he no longer hated Black people. He said the Jews were the enemy of Black people and White people. He wanted to know if I would join with him against the Jews.

Also, while searching for the link to *The Klan on Trial*, I came across another episode I had no idea existed. It was a follow-up to the murder of Mrs. Corporon's family, and it too left out any association with the Moore County Prison or Bobby Person.

The exploitation by the Southern Poverty Law Center did not end with changing what happened at the Moore County Prison to a story about one man. The SPLC and others profited at the expense of Klan victims. Morris Dees and the SPLC demanded the money sent to Bobby Person by donors.

In 1992, Morris sent out thank you letters to donors as if Bobby Person had written the letters. Morris had Bobby sign the donor letter and return it to him. He told Bobby that donors would be sending money to him, and he should endorse the checks and send the checks back to him along with the cash. Being grateful for the help from the SPLC, Bobby complied. Enough letters to fill a laundry basket came weekly for years. When I returned to NC in 2001, Bobby was still receiving laundry baskets full of letters and money.

People on the Left can commit the very act they are accusing others of and get away with it. We saw that during the Summer of Love riots and January 6 protesters. We saw it in the persecution of Kyle Rittenhouse as rioters walked free. Those of us the Left sees as enemies do not seem able to gain politically from the greed and exploitation the Left puts on display daily. Exposing the Left's complicity with racists will give them something to explain to those Americans who are easily exploited by the left. Once there is no White Guilt, millions will be free to end the power vacuum. Conservatives and Republicans, as well as all Americans, will be free of this long racial nightmare.

Exposing the Left does not mean racism will be ending. However, it will mean that racism as a tool will be ending, laws will be enforced, and the Constitution will live again. With this as the norm, there will be no need for civil rights organizations that abandoned their mission more than a half-century ago. It will also mean their Race Card has been declined.

Almost 35 years after the Jet Magazine article/cover-up, I posted the following Facebook message on October 20, 2020.

> *Several weeks ago, I offered $1000.00 if Trump has done more racial harm to Black people than Democrats. I even said you can leave off the White Democrats. Had I been challenged; I was just going to put up this little article from*

Jet Magazine. This was the total coverage in the Black press of what was the biggest victory over the Klan in US history. So, you can put up all that I just voted, riding with Biden or my ancestors died for me. I know your truth.

The post was in response to Facebook friends calling Trump a racist nonstop. In response to the criticism, I offered the reward of $1000 if Democrats had a better civil rights record than Trump. To make it easier for them, later I excluded the White Democrats and still had no takers. After I showed how I would prove it, Family members and friends who offered no help and stayed silent while Bobby and I alone fought racism at the prison and the Klan in Bobby's yard are now outraged. The people who call Black people Toms, Sellouts, and White Supremacists had their opportunity to fight hate and racism but chose to show that bravery on Facebook.

The EEOC's Racist Quid Pro Quo

The first time I heard the term "Political Patronage Mill," it was used in a negative reference that described employees at the EEOC. America's biggest unkept secret is that the EEOC is corrupt. I learned through lawyers, civil right activists, and personal experience that the EEOC was inept because the agency is staffed with people who worked in political campaigns. They were given these government jobs as a reward. If one wants to know how Corporate America suddenly became "Woke," start with discrimination filings at the EEOC and follow the evidence back to civil rights organizations like the BLM, NAACP, and the LGBTQ+ community. There you will find many instances of something for something.

The Left protest racism everywhere in America except the workplace. For reasons that will become apparent, the Left sees no kinship between racism and discrimination. In most cases, it's not the racism that cripples victims; it's the legal process.

Corporate America's "wokeness" went public in Atlanta on April 2, 2021. On that date, Major League Baseball canceled the All-

Star Game in Atlanta. In spite of the feeble pleas from former gubernatorial candidate Stacy Abrams not to relocate the games, corporations like Delta Airlines, Coca Cola, and other companies joined Major League Baseball in a woke exit. This announcement seems to be following a trend that continues today. Companies that have always been Conservatives seem to have become woke overnight.

Keep what you just read in mind as you read the following. In 1984 and 2021, two government investigations uncovered the fact that the EEOC was not "fully" investigating discrimination claims. Despite this finding, most news outlets who reported this story blamed the problem on a lack of staffing and funding. Even in the era of Cancel Culture, civil rights groups, including women and Gay groups, are yet to protest the abuse the government admits exists. Add to that the donation and advertising dollars the civil rights industry and the media received from their new friends, corporations, and we have a quid pro quo.

****

Government agencies that police racism, civil rights groups, along with organizations that report the news are co-conspirators. People who control these organizations are paid to shift racism from corporations and the rich to the police, then to poor and working-class White Conservatives. Coca Cola even paid the NAACP millions of dollars to call people racist who opposed removing surgery drinks from the food stamp list. This same quid pro quo, more than anything, is behind forcing people to get the jab, firings, and other politically correct mandates.

Now we know that the EEOC, the media, civil rights groups, and the Democrat Party protect and blackmail corporations in exchange for revenue and other favors. We know from the lack of protest and news coverage that corruption is widespread; that it has existed for over a half-century, and the sin covers many corrupt people. Even worse, it all takes place with the blessing and support of most African Americans who scream about racism daily. These woke African Americans actively work to whitewash any racism prominent African Americans benefit from regardless of the cost to Black America, the LGBTQ+ community, other protected groups, and society

Currently, this country is undergoing a racial overhaul to wipe out so-called systemic racism. During this racial overhaul, individuals have been canceled for racial slurs made when they were ten years old. While woke groups are busy canceling Americans, documented racial discrimination cases made by victims under oath are ignored, and the government is one of the abusers.

In a country where one hears racism charges every day, EEOC filings and convictions seem to be at odds with the EEOC findings. The EEOC finds discrimination in less than 10% of the complaints. That 10% or less EEOC finding represents complicity and abuse. We know from government investigations that abuses at the EEOC are widely known about; moreover, I know from my own experience that the EEOC is corrupt.

Consider this. Between 1997 and 2020, victims alleging discrimination filed 67,000 to 91,000 racial, sex, and other workplace violations each year. In all those years, the EEOC found fault in less than 10% of cases. Add that dismal finding to the two Government Accounting Office investigations that found that the EEOC was not fully investigating charges. From the GAO investigation alone, it is public knowledge that the abusive practice goes back at least to 1984. No protest here from those who bail out rioters and looters.

During that 23-year period, almost two million civil rights complaints were filed against employers. There have been no *60 Minutes* reports, no Al Sharpton protest, and the "Squad" is too busy labeling Republicans as racist. There have been no investigations, no headlines, or protest. Businesses have more racism charges against them than all other racial complaints against Republicans, and all those White Supremacists Joe Biden claimed are everywhere. However, to help keep racism in the news and away from the EEOC, the civil rights community created "Karens" and everything Karens do and say is covered daily by the media. Fast forward to today and you will understand why businesses are enforcing the unconstitutional mandates of the Left and the government. One can see evidence through the lack of enforcement that ties Corporate America and the press to ANTIFA BLM's bank accounts and the ability to redefine rioting.

On a segment of the *Tucker Carlson Show* that aired on April 12, 2021, Tucker asked Candice Owens why Corporations were pumping money into groups like BLM and ANTIFA. Tucker Carlson wanted to know what was in it for Corporate America. Responding, Candice stated that corporations want to run the country. While that is true, there are other reasons that are more compelling, just in case elections don't work out.

The Left wants to control the country, and corporations want cheap labor and employees who are not likely to file discrimination complaints. This orgy of greed and the lust for power have created a permanent Black underclass who get nothing other than exploitation. The need to deflect from this is the reason for the borders crisis, firing people over vaccine shots, gender pronouns, and children mutilation. This is the reason wokeness is so extreme. To use the Judge Judy analogy: If things don't make sense, something bigger is going on.

The role the press plays cannot be understated. Consider the May 14, 2021, article from Forbes Magazine: "1,000 Cuts: The Toll Of Racism In The Workplace". I cite this article to reaffirm that, in the "everything is racist" era, racism in the workplace is being ignored. If you read the article, you are left with this question: How does an article about the harm from workplace racism become a story in part about Black men's fear of calling the police?

That article cited as contributors Soledad O'Brien and Laura LeBleu, two Far Left Zealots who fit Dr. King's description as having: *"… a degree of academic and economic security and because in some ways they profit... have become insensitive to the problems of the masses."* Instead of describing the toll racism takes in the workplace, their thesis sentence for the article was the following: *A fresh take from diversity leaders on how to take meaningful action.* Nowhere in the article do O'Brien and LeBleu mention the fact that racism in the workplace creates a hostile work environment for protected groups. The diversity training they cite is not the remedy for workplace discrimination. The remedy for workplace discrimination is Punitive Damages. This article confirms that the "Woke" press and other social justice warriors are in a racist racketeering scheme with Corporate America.

The very people demanding an end to racism and promising to burn down America have made a deal with Corporate America. The media, the civil rights industry, women's groups, and the LGBTQ+ community have agreed to let Corporate America commit workplace racism and other forms of discrimination unabated. It is also clear that this quid quo pro is behind censoring, spying on Americans, and canceling those who the Left opposes. The evidence is in the behavior of the EEOC, the media, and civil rights leaders. Another reason that Corporate America is "woke" is that they do not want to be sued for reparations or pay all the victims the EEOC abused on their behalf.

Thanks to people like Soledad O'Brien and Laura LeBleu. Corporate America is not only "Woke but protected." There have been millions of workplace discrimination complaints filed against employers in America. Yet, there have been no new laws, no demands to increase funding for the EEOC, no press, and no protest, ever. Today racism is underpinning a plethora of manufactured social justice issues and political campaigns. The only difference is BLM is doing the shakedown rather than Al Sharpton and Jesse Jackson. Unlike Al Sharpton, BLM has a political agenda, whereas Big Al and

Jesse just want to pad their pockets and avoid back taxes.

Corporate America is donating, or I should say investing billions of dollars in groups who are burning and looting. These groups avoid providing or insisting that the government give free lawyers to help employees sue for discrimination. The evidence of this relationship is more evident in the 2020 Equal Employment Opportunity Commission's (EEOC) Charging Statistics. The exchange of something for something is very apparent; it is the reason corporations are "woke" and supporting the goals of the "woke" movement.

Based on the EEOC Charge Statistics, over the last 20 years, more than 1.5 million people filed Title VII complaints with the EEOC. Civil rights organizations," including women's and gay groups, have sat idle as the Rules of Evidence were whittled down to the point where a company almost has to admit they discriminated for someone to win at the EEOC or in court. Between the two-year wait time and the malfeasance, it is less frustrating and less harmful to skip the EEOC, ask for a Right to Sue letter, and head to court without a lawyer.

The following news article and CBO investigations highlight the abuse at the EEOC and gives the reasons why people are avoiding the EEOC.

> More and more workplace discrimination cases are being closed before they're even investigated
> By Maryam Jameel Jun 14, 2019, 9:30 am EDT
> *Co-published in partnership with the Center for Public Integrity*
> Backlogs should not matter when it comes to the quality of

their investigative work. Even if a case takes three years, you should be treated fairly. It's a classic Washington catch-22: For years, Congress has chastised the agency that investigates workplace discrimination for its unwieldy backlog of unresolved cases while giving it little to no extra money to address the problem.
In turn, officials at the US Equal Employment Opportunity Commission have found a workaround: Close more cases without investigating them.
https://www.vox.com/identities/2019/6/14/18663296/congress-eeoc-workplace-discrimination

The people who are transforming America over the issue of race are comfortable with this abuse. The news media's self-incriminating words are indictments against them and the "woke" mob. The press report government corruption that the government admits to and then offers no relief for the victims of the corruption they report. Where are those headlines? Not having headlines that indict Corporate America may explain why CNN's ratings are in the tank, and they can still pay Joy Reid, Don Lemon, and others millions in salary with no one watching. People who want news that validates what they believe make good consumers. This might explain why CNN refuses to change its business model to attract more viewers. From a commercial revenue point of view, a few hundred thousand rabid viewers are more valuable than having millions of free-thinking viewers.

****

Rather than demand reparations from corporations and the government, civil rights groups and the Left are blaming the police, Conservatives, and America for acts of racism they are participating in and making possible. Their remedy for the injustice and racism Black people have suffered at their hands is to demand money for what slaves went through. Only someone who lusts for power and money would ignore the liability of the EEOC and the corporations and seek damages for slavery

As previously noted, the GAO's investigation found that the EEOC harmed victims of discrimination in the workplace. The civil rights industry and the press were handed this information, and they ignored it as if it were a Hunter Biden crime. The evidence is verifiable, and the EEOC is part of the protection racket according to the General Accounting Office:

> *Since 2008, the EEOC has doubled the share of complaints involving companies or local government agencies that it places on its lowest-priority track, effectively guaranteeing no probes, mediation, or other substantive efforts on behalf of those workers. About 30 percent of cases were shunted to that category last year, according to internal data obtained by the Center for Public Integrity through a public records request.* https:// https://www.gao.gov/assets/hrd-89-11.pdf

This mistreatment of complaints is far more recent than slavery. Therefore, if anyone is entitled to reparations, it is the victims who went to the EEOC for help. Unlike slavery, EEOC victims are of all colors.

Conservatives, Republicans, and Black Americans who are sick and tired of the name-calling need to use this information to take the civil rights issue away from the press, the Left, and Democrats. We can start with the racist practice of the EEOC assigning minority investigators to victims seeking help. The EEOC does this for cover, particularly in high-profile cases. All the victims of their illegal practice must act. Otherwise, African Americans who participated in racism against Black people may get a reparation check for slavery. Now that Corporate America is "woke," let them and the civil rights groups who protected the corporations pick up their share of the reparation tab because no one benefitted more.

We know from the investigations on the previous pages that the EEOC did not thoroughly investigate charges. Ricardo Jones was a Senior Federal Investigator for the EEOC and blew the whistle long before the GAO investigations. In his lawsuit, Jones raised the very issues the GAO had found the EEOC guilty of. Although this practice had been going on through Democrat and Republican Presidencies, Ricardo Jones' lawsuit against the EEOC awaited the First African American President. However, now that there is an African American President, fairness and justice have become reduced to the statement "he's not the President of Black people!" Justice now meant that Ricardo Jones' lawsuit had to be sealed by the court to ensure no protest and no whistleblower status for Ricardo Jones. President Obama, taking a cue from the EEOC's, "Black on Black" playbook, appointed Jacqueline Berrien, former NAACP Legal Defense, and Educational Fund, Associate Director-Counsel, to head the EEOC. One of her first official acts was to fire Ricardo Jones.

https://ricohenry7.wordpress.com/2011/03/22/ricardo-jones-v-jacqueline-berrien-et-al-eeoc-fraud-against-the-public/

The title of this book makes the claim that, more often than not, the racist looks like the victim. And the title also corroborates the fact that complicity racism is and always will be an essential part of the construction of racism. The 2008 lawsuit filed by Ricardo Jones, a Black American, against Jacqueline Berrien, Director of the EEOC, who is African American, shows the same widespread complicity that existed when Bobby and I sued the NCDOC and the KKK. The appointment of MS Berrien also gave plausible deniability to President Obama. Few Americans knew it at the time, but there was a growing movement to pressure President Obama to do something about the EEOC, but the weight of history was too powerful.

The Killing Fields of Robeson County

Most Americans know of Montgomery because of the Bus Boycott, Selma because of Bloody Sunday, Oklahoma because of the massacre, and Kenosha because of George Floyd. On the other hand, the public knows little or nothing about the racism and murder that took place in Robeson County, North Carolina. Racism and murder in this county are the one place the press and those who exploit avoid even pretending to offer help. In the 1980s, I found myself knee-deep in hate and betrayal while protesting racism and racist murder in Robeson County.

The notoriety from lawsuits against the prison and the Klan gave Bobby and me enough prominence to be welcomed into the non-legacy civil rights community. As community activists, we protested and organized in Robeson County and across the South. Bobby and I became board members of (NCARRV) North Carolinians Against Racist and Religious Violence. We served on NCARRV's board with NAACP State Director Carolyn Coleman, LGBTQ author, activist Mabs Segrest, Leah Wise, head of Southerners for Economic Justice, and Jim Grant from Black Workers for Justice. We were also the lead plaintiffs in the ACLU lawsuit to redraw Moore County, North Carolina voting districts.

Bobby and I organized and protested racism across North Carolina and beyond. Some of the people we organized with were NC Supreme court Justice Anita Earl and now Congresswoman Alma Adams when they were building their civil rights resumes. Our alliance with these ambitious warriors had us protesting against racism and racist murder, in Robeson County and elsewhere.

Bobby and I first went to Robeson County after the Robbins, North Carolina chapter of the NAACP sold us out. The President of the Robbins chapter invited Black officers from the Moore County Prison to their monthly meeting to discuss the racial issue at the prison. Eddie Lane, Bobby, and I were the only officers to show up. We sat there unrecognized as they got all of their business out of the way. Without notice, they decided to adjourn the meeting with us sitting there unheard.

****

Before they could close the meeting, the wife of officer Eddie Lane stood up and spoke. She asked why they would invite us to the meeting and then close it as if we were not there. Although this chapter was in the same county, their excuse was that they could not help us because we did not belong to their chapter. In the end, they refused to help us and wrapped up their meeting with the suggestion that we contact Emory Little, President of the Moore County chapter of the NAACP. Bobby and I ran into this same conflict of interest with Emory Little and the NAACP President in Robeson County. Both NAACP Presidents were ready to throw us under the bus.

Emery Little asked the NAACP's Robeson County Legal Counsel, Angus Boaz Thompson, to investigate our discrimination complaint against the NCDOC. After visiting his office in Lumberton, Attorney Thompson told us we had an excellent case. He asked us to go back home and write everything down, then return in two weeks. When Bobby and I returned, he said that we did not have a case and suggested the harassment, cross-burning, and discrimination was White men joking around. Later on, Mr. Thompson would represent Daniel Green, the man who murdered James Jordan, the father of Michael Jordan of the NBA fame. Now we know why the Black man took the fall.

Bobby and I returned to Robeson County again as protesting board members of North Carolinians Against Racist and Religious Violence (NCARRV). We were part of a multi-racial protest planned in St Paul, NC, to address racism, unsolved police shootings, and Klan murders in Robeson County. The excerpt below, from Mabs Segrest's book, *Memoir of a Race Traitor*, sets the stage:

> Two weeks later, I drove to a meeting of citizens concerned to respond to Mrs. Sinclair's death. I stopped by Moore County to pick up Jimmy Pratt and Bobby Person, Board members who had brought the Klanwatch suit against the White Patriots. I was not eager to travel these back roads by myself at night. The church was full, the audience mostly Black. Jimmy and Bobby spent most of the night outside standing guard. When I was introduced, I explained what I knew about the extensive Klan activity in the area and offered NCARRV's help. In

the months following this meeting, however, community response dissipated. Local law enforcement kept saying they had a "prime suspect," but they never arrested anyone for the murder.

The protest planned at that meeting took place on Easter Monday, April 19, 1987. The Easter protest was attended by Amnesty International and boycotted by every civil rights group in the country. Although Ms. Sinclair's murder fit the White on Black racial narrative the press and civil rights groups preferred, in their eyes, there were Democrats to protect. Therefore, the press coverage was minimal, and the later coverage was forced at gunpoint, as I will explain later. For Ms. Sinclair, there would be no celebrity treatment like that received by Sandra Bland and Breonna Taylor,

The Easter Monday protest coalesced around the racist rape and murder of Joyce Sinclair. Ms. Sinclair had just become the first Black person promoted to a supervisory position at Burlington Industries, a textile company. Her young daughter told police a White man dressed in white had kidnapped her. Authorities found Ms. Sinclair's body at the site where a Klan rally had previously been held. The Medical Examiner determined she had been raped and murdered. The man who raped and murdered her has never been brought to justice. The police have a suspect but have made no arrest in 40+ years. No one, including Black Lives Matter, is interested in making Ms. Sinclair's racist rape and murder part of any Critical Race Theory.

The Left is busy canceling everyone and demanding reparations going back to 1619. Ms. Sinclair's death in Robeson

County is treated as if helping good people fight for justice may uncover something the Left wants to stay hidden. Not one person from the civil rights legacy groups attended or endorsed the march. For Ms. Sinclair there was no Jesse Jackson and no Al Sharpton. The NAACP openly boycotted the protest and tried to cancel it. If memory serves me, even the program *America's Most Wanted* turned its back on this one.

Weeks before the protest, Robeson County NAACP President Rev. WM Cooper sent out a press statement saying the NAACP would not be participating in the march and ordered his members not to attend. He also told those of us who were non-members not to come, because the NAACP was not getting us out of jail. Not long after the march, the press, who were silent about the murders in Robeson County, were forced, as I mentioned, to report what people were protesting at the point of a gun. Eddie Hatcher and Tim Jacobs, two Native Americans, took the staff of the Robesonian newspaper hostage. Their demand, in return for the release of hostages, was an investigation into the unsolved murders of Blacks and Native Americans in Robeson County.

Shortly after the protest, the father of basketball superstar Michael Jordan came along and parked to rest. He, too, joined the growing list of people murdered in Robeson County. Based on all the things I had experienced, the murder of James Jordan, was only going to lead to more cover-ups. The press refusal to properly investigate and report on the murders before the James Jordan case had already provided the first hint that a more extensive cover-up was coming.

The second clue was Daniel Greene's court-appointed attorney Angus Boaz Thompson. He was the attorney that sold Bobby and me out. When I found out that Mr. Thompson was Greene's lawyer, I knew Daniel Greene would be the scapegoat. My reasoning was that the death of a person of James Jordan's notoriety might invite freelance journalists or people who might discover more of what was going on in Robeson County. Therefore, the press and civil rights leaders had to do more deflecting. To the rescue, there came the Race Baiters to soak up the news by starting a conspiracy about one man.

After James Jordan's decomposed body was found floating in a South Carolina creek by the police in McColl, Jesse Jackson, the press, and other civil rights leaders tried to make a race issue out of what they believed was a "hasty cremation." Jackson and others claimed the coroner should have known James Jordan was a prominent Black man from his expensive dental work. The Chicago Tribune, reporting on the cremation, wrote:

> Rev. Jesse Jackson, among others, suggested the cremation was either a "cover-up" or "disrespect" for black men. Though some experts do not totally discount the possibility of racism, they say a less sinister explanation is just as likely: that it is yet another mishandled unnatural death in a nation where such is commonplace.
> https://www.chicagotribune.com/news/ct-xpm-1993-08-17-9308170101-story.html

The same media and civil rights leaders that now see racism and a cover-up everywhere else, cannot see racism and a cover-up on a much larger scale in the same place. By the time James Jordan was murdered in Robeson County, there had been protests against the rape and murder of Black people and Native Americans in Robeson County off and on for almost ten years. Under different circumstances, the murder of James Jordan would have been a death penalty case in Robeson County, but it was not. I note this because Joe Freeman Britt, the retired District Attorney, is in the Guinness Book of Records for sending more people to Death Row than anyone.

His son prosecuted this case, and I'm sure that this is a record the Britt family is proud of and that they want to keep in the family. However, the robbery and execution of James Jordan was not deemed to be a death penalty case.

As I previously stated, Daniel Green was the scapegoat, because there was also the possibility of Native American protest, and of the intrusion of independent and foreign journalists. It was easier to buy off Black leaders than suppress all the publicity from prosecuting or executing Larry Demery, a Native American. After all, Black on Black murder is acceptable – even if the murder victim is the father of a celebrity – and the Left needed to deflect. Once the NAACP's President was bribed with a county job, protest in Robeson County virtually stopped.

Daniel Greene has always maintained his innocence, and there has been no shortage of people who believe he was railroaded for a crime he didn't commit. An October 2021 podcast is telling his story. (Follow the Truth on Apple Podcasts} As you will see, the usual social justice vultures are circling overhead or maybe even producing the podcast.

For those of us familiar with Robeson County, we know life there is as cheap as Black life in Chicago. Robeson County's population, at that time, was one-third White, one-third Black, and one-third Native American. However, Whites were in charge, and minority candidates who ran for office were often shot before the election. Even with all the corruption, police shootings, and racism, the media, to this day, is still uninterested. They ignored the murders in Robeson as if it was Chicago. That is until another murder came along that needed deflecting.

The rape and murder of 13-year-old Hania Aguilar in 2016 sent the press into cover-up mode yet again. Given Robeson County's history of racism, Klan violence, and police shootings, one would think the press would use it as a back story or infer that Hania Aguilar's murder may have been racially motivated. Since Hania Aguilar was Hispanic and her father had been deported, the press turned its attention to Trump's Wall and ignored all those unsolved racially motivated murders and protest in Robeson County. In many ways, there are many similarities between fighting racism at the Moore County Prison and fighting racism in Robeson County. The two situations share the same conspirators; the NAACP, and the press come to mind.

The First Tuesday after Sunday

In 2020, a Rasmussen poll of all Americans found that: *"Americans Say African Americans More Racist Than Whites, Hispanics, Asians."* Even African Americans and Black people named African Americans the most racist in the same poll.

How did a race of people who marched and died fighting racism become a race of people full of hate, blame, and abandonment? Is this a case of hate producing hate? The answer to this enigma comes on the First Tuesday after Sunday in every election year. To most Americans, the first Tuesday in November is Election Day, and Sunday is a day of worship. The First Tuesday after Sunday represents the conflict between the two days, which is why it has turned African Americans into a hate group, leading to a day of reckoning for all Black Americans.

The day of reckoning, for all of Black America, was shepherded in riding the behavior of a solitary group. Throughout this book, I have referred to that group as "Woke" African Americans and sometimes as the D.A.A.M people (Democrat African American Majority). Their leaders control the voice and destiny of most Black Americans. They have churches on almost every corner, and the elites control the Black media, civil rights organizations, and every educational institution.

African American Democrat leaders are backed up by an army of people acting like timid shivering chattel. They rule over Black America like an army of goose-stepping jackbooted thugs. The D.A.A.M people's loyalty is not to their God or their race. Their loyalty is to a single political party and its warped ideology. The people who obey and follow corrupt leaders identify politically and ideologically as African Americans Democrat Christians. They separate themselves from Black people who are Conservative, Christian or both. African American Democrats claim to be Christian, 364 days a year (except Leap Years). On that one day in November, they do not love their race, neighbor, or God. On that one day, they are Democrat Voting Stock.

Woke African Americans are not Marxists. They are Christians in case there is a God. They are not Baptist, African Methodist Episcopal, or Presbyterian. They are Democrats. Their God is not the God of Abraham, Moses, or Jesus. Their God is always the head of the Democrat Party. Their marching orders come from the Democrat Party, and those orders are obeyed over the laws of God. For example, if African American ministers preach from their pulpit that God is against a particular sin and Obama or the Democratic Party is for it, they go with Obama and the Democrat Party. Woke African American Christians never side with Conservative Christians. They always side with the people who hate God. This act alone separates African Americans from God, and that has consequences.

I once read somewhere that accepting what most people believe to be real is a familiar measure of sanity in any society. That was my definition of sanity until I read Dr. King's speech on what hate does to a person or group that hates. He said, "…when you hate, you can't think straight… Your objectivity is gone…There is nothing more tragic to see than a person whose heart is filled with hate…." The people filled with taught hatred are so dominant in the Black culture that logical, rational thinking, and good behavior are no longer group practice. In this case, when in Rome, doing what the Romans do is insanity. When Bobby Person and I filed a lawsuit that affected the Democrat Party, I found out that accepting what the majority in the community believed to be real was insanity. African Americans had gone insane and wanted us to join the insanity.

Because I did not join the unthinking, I could now see what I had been blind to for years. There are consequences for all Black Americans when the majority chose politics over the God they claim to worship. When that happens, one does not know whether to scratch their wrist or wind their butts or, as Dr. King put it, end up "…laughing when they should be crying. And crying when they should be laughing." They are wandering in an intellectual desert for the same reason God left the Hebrew slaves in the desert. That is, to die off.

African Americans who are filled with political hatred have turned our culture into something resembling Bizarro World from the Superman comics. Sometime after the Black Power Movement, everything in Black America became the exact opposite of everything elsewhere. What we had once believed was good became bad, and bad became good. These are not the "we shall overcome" people of the civil rights era or the people of the Black Power movement. These African Americans wield their woke politics like a two-edged sword. What they do to their community on Election Day has the effect of a plague of locusts from hell.

They are even more hate-filled when other Black Americans file anti-discrimination complaints. In my experience, for filing lawsuits, protesting, and now writing about what happened to me at the hands of African Americans, I am despised, an Uncle Tom, and a Sellout. The biggest sin I committed was to hold Black American leaders responsible for what they had done, and not blame every White person in history instead.

It is important to understand that African Americans follow a well-defined narrative. If one holds them responsible for things they are doing to each other, you have to balance it with something Whites are doing to Whites or Whites are doing to Black people. If all of this sounds like déjà vu, that is because we are reliving it again in 2023. Liberals are putting into place rules that allow African Americans to rob and harm others, because of some past injustice by White Americans.

African Americans came this far by the grace of God and the sacrifices of God-inspired people. So how did they come to care so little about the God they claim and the people who helped Black people survive? For example, at the Moore County School Board meeting in October 2021, a 69-year-old African American man told the board that nothing has changed in his 69 years on Earth. This man has seen no progress in having a right to vote, the death of Jim Crow, or the election of a Black President. He pays no reverence to people who have sacrificed so he could stand before the school board with a Black elected member and complain. Nor do he reference the 350,000 White soldiers who died fighting in the Civil War, partly on behalf of his ancestors and him. Being ungrateful is the attitude of the Woke African Americans I know.

The lack of gratitude is why the African American community has come to the point where they freely choose to support the people who exploit Black people over saving their children. I believe that being this ungrateful has led African Americans to the same fate as the Hebrew slaves Moses bought out of bondage in Egypt. If we could separate the demographics of Black Conservatives from African Americans, the things African American Democrats have done to hurt the Black race would be apparent. This is why living in Black America today is like living in reruns of the Ten Commandments.

The history of the Hebrew slaves is not alone in being relevant to African Americans' ungodly behavior. Black people didn't receive Ten Commandments when slavery ended. However, later on the government commissioned a study called the Moynihan Report. This report spelled out the coming crises to Black Americans. And yet, as a race, we refused to heed. Nor did we offer any resistance when the Left used the report as a training manual to exploit African Americans for their vote. This report is a damning indictment of the way they turned African Americans into racists.

Black people before becoming "Woke" were described in the Moynihan Report this way:

> That the Negro American has survived at all is
> extraordinary—a lesser people might simply
> have died out, as indeed others have. That the
> Negro community has not only survived, but
> in this political generation has entered national
> affairs as a moderate, humane, and
> constructive national force is the highest
> testament to the healing powers of the
> democratic ideal and the creative vitality of the

Negro people.

In a 2012 poll, many of the people and their grandchildren cited in the Moynihan Report were described this way:

> Nearly three-fourths of black men and two-thirds of black women "strongly agree" with the sentence "I see myself as someone who has high self-esteem." By comparison, 59 percent of white men, and fewer than half of white women strongly agree.
>
> Similarly, black men and women say they're less stressed. Fewer than a third of black men say they "frequently" experience stress, compared to 44 percent of white men. Four in ten black women frequently experience stress, yet just over half of white women say the same.
>
> Black Americans: Less Stress, More Self-Esteem, Yet More Worries? | HuffPost

The only way the 2012 self-esteem poll makes any sense is that African Americans became racist during the Obama Administration. I saw the same high level of self-esteem belief in the Klansmen I spent years fighting at work. Like members of the Klan, African Americans today call people stupid, ignorant and make up all kinds of racial stereotypes to harm others and justify that harm. Both African Americans and the Klan act alike, and they should, because both African Americans and the Klan have their creator's DNA. The Democrat Party created both groups, along with Critical Race Theory.

When Patrick Moynihan drafted his report, almost eighty-five percent of black households were two-parent families. The ability to predict the consequences of behavior a century before it happens is both suspicious and enlightening when taking into consideration Black Lives Matter came along to do away with the Black family. BLM is Armageddon-scale evil, for those who chose the First Tuesday over Sunday.

African Americans separated themselves from God and returned to Pharaoh, the Democrat Party, without a thank you to the people who had brought Black people out of bondage. This behavior is behind Black people's inability to rise as a group. This behavior, more than any reason given by politicians, social scientists, or the Moynihan Report, is why Black Americans suffer disproportionately in the land of opulence. Consider health, death, education, and economic statistics. When these statistics are dire, African Americans are over-represented. At fault is the Woke African American majority who chose their politics over God. Because of their behavior, Woke African Americans, unlike Black Conservatives, are not respected; instead, they are considered by other groups in America and the world to be the most racist.

African Americans who enter the workplace with an attitude that employers owe them something are one of the reason employers want immigrants of color to replace Woke employees of color. On the way to accommodate this desire is a multitude of black and brown immigrants who can see a path to success even if the only job they can get is cutting the grass of disgruntled African Americans. I cannot comprehend why African Americans cannot see what all those Black and brown illegal immigrants see. Instead of having their eyes opened, African Americans, stripped of a sense of self-preservation are paving the way for immigrants to replace them in the workplace and at the ballot box. Consider this article from Breitbart:

> *Black Americans who spent most of their lives working on Mississippi farms are suing their former employer after they were replaced by foreign workers on the H-2A visa program.*

Black Americans Sue U.S. Farms for Replacing Them with Foreigners (breitbart.com)

****

Unlike African Americans, immigrants, and the LGBTQ+ community are using the 1964 Civil Rights Bill, our history of racism, and African Americans' political power to make their demands on the Democrat Party. African Americans demand nothing and get nothing from Democrats in return. Remember the young illegal immigrant Hispanic girl who followed Senator Kyrsten Sinema into the bathroom? She did not do it out of gratitude for the African Americans who made it possible, at their own expense. As an illegal immigrant, she was doing more for her race with that trip to the bathroom than African Americans did with a Black President aided by a filibuster-proof Democrat Congress.

Illegal Immigrants and the LGBTQ+ community owe the fact they have more rights than any natural-born American to African Americans and their tribal leaders. Instead of collecting on that debt, leaders in the Black community are continuing their tradition of manipulating the Black community to benefit everyone but Black people. They have a free hand to pave the way for black and brown immigrants on behalf of the Left and big business.

Long before African Americans turned the Black community into a self-fulfilling prophecy, so-called Black leaders had plundered the Great Society Program, lost the war on poverty, and squandered an entire civil rights victory. Left in the wake of this is a race of ungrateful people who are unworthy of and unable to produce or accept leaders like Dr. King and Malcolm X anymore. Nor can they produce, through birth, a Berry Gordy or, through freedom of expression, another Harlem Renaissance.

****

African Americans could not advance even after electing a Black man President because they turned him into a God. In the eight years of Obama's Presidency, they did not make a single demand. Right now, six years after Obama's presidency, African Americans, in spite of all their political power, still have not made a demand on any legislature or President. The inability to make demands on behalf of their community and its children is happening because, all the things Liberal African Americans say "Amen" to every Sunday, they undo on the following Tuesday in November at the polls.

What follows this betrayal of God and the laws of survival are consequences. Unlike the past, a merciful God did not leave the American slaves in a desert to die off. Nor did God give African Americans Ten Commandments to keep them straight. Instead, God gave American slaves free will. When slavery ended, American slaves built communities, institutions of learning, and businesses. Rather than build on that success, their descendants have abused that legacy by being disobedient and ungrateful. They chose a political party over God, and the consequences have been generational. African American Democrats who call themselves Christians have passed down misery like a biblical plague, and that plague landed on our children.

Like the Arc of the Moral Universe, the Bible bends towards justice. Many of the prophecies from the Bible have been fulfilled in Black America. The book of Exodus 20:5 is a prophecy visible today:

> *Thou shalt not bow down thyself to them, nor serve them: for I, the LORD thy God am a jealous God, visiting the iniquity of the fathers upon the children unto the third and fourth generation of them that hate me.*

****

In a culture where everything is racist, Black children catch Hell for the misbehavior of the adults. There is zero support among African American Democrats for those who want to call attention to the plight of Black children. The Klan spent more than 100 years trying to accomplish what Woke African American Democrats did to Black people between the elections of the first African American President and the election of Joe Biden.

Notwithstanding, since 1973, there have been more than 20 million abortions and 400,000 murders with barely a protest. In Baltimore, none of the 23 schools come up to proficiency standards in reading and math. Ignoring Black kids has become the paradigm anywhere that the African American vote makes the difference in an election. Rather than demand better schools and teachers, African

Americans supported Oregon's law removing basic literacy and math standards for Black students to graduate. Promoting students this way is not what Bush meant by "No Child Left Behind," but they have chosen it anyway. After years of protest and death to end segregation, Liberal colleges allowed Black students to live in segregated dorms and have separate graduations. Rather than calling this conduct teaching, Americans should call it child abuse. or madness

Furthermore, consider the silence around White Leftist/Progressives teachers and other schools teaching Black kids that good conduct and not being disruptive in class are signs of White Supremacy. This new discipline compounds matters because "acting White" is already a tool used by African Americans to limit the intellectual growth of Black people.

African American Democrats see no racism in the things I just laid out. However, they did see White Supremacy in the form of a "dog whistle" when a Conservative Black woman became the first Black woman to become the Lieutenant Governor of Virginia, the former capital of the Confederacy.

I read somewhere that Black kids are treated as nothing, and everything around them reinforces it. In their community, Black kids are accused of not listening, being hardheaded, disrespectful, gang bangers, and thugs by the adults who taught them the behavior. It's always something or someone else's fault. It would be nice if adults shouldered the same responsibility as the children they accuse of being irresponsible. The following excerpt on Black young adults is factual. I agree with the premise. However, I see it as art imitating life. The late Dr. Frances Cress Welsing did not go far enough:

> "We're the only people on this entire planet who've been taught to sing and praise our demeanment (calling ourselves bit*hes, ho*s, dogs and nias)... If you can train people to demean and degrade themselves, you can oppress them forever. You can even program them to kill themselves, and they won't even understand what happened."

In this excerpt from an article by Dr. E. Faye Williams titled "Eliminate Demeanment", published in the Richmond Free Times, Dr. Williams' use of the term "we're" and "we've" is used to place the blame collectively. Where was the "demeanment" charge when Rev. Lyons, Rev. Al Sharpton, Rev. Jackson, and a rapacious leadership class set these examples?

In the case below, it is Corporate America she holds responsible. Dr. Williams writes in the same article:

> We recognize there are black franchisees of McDonald's and Subway restaurants, but that's not a good reason for accepting the disrespect of our people. Franchise owners should be the first in line influencing their corporate offices to spend their advertising dollars on programs that uplift us. Franchise owners don't get a pass just because they want to earn a dollar off the very community they should be uplifting...."

The Black community has churches on every corner. You can reach out into the dark and touch a preacher. There are more than 5,000 elected African Americans and far too many civil rights organizations to count. These elected and self-appointed representatives are in addition to the many African Americans who own broadcast stations, sports teams, and other businesses. Yet, the uplifting of the Black community is left to corporate handouts and Black children are left to their fate, with no help from the African American vote.

Since 2013, I have been copying arguments from individuals in chat groups like Michael Baisden and Facebook. In the 10 years since, I did not get a single African American or White Liberal to support a Black issue in all those years. They acted as though the murders in Chicago were some "Right-Wing" Talking Point that never happened. However, when it looked like the prosecution's case in the Kyle Rittenhouse trial was going badly, African Americans were all over cable news and social media supporting the criminals who had been trying to murder a 17-year-old innocent White kid. They even changed the Bible and claimed God supports abortion. These same people will defend DACA and support made-to-order trans children. They will give all their support to others while abandoning their own children.

The African American majority forgets the contributions of young Black Americans to the arts and the struggle for social justice. In the sixties and seventies, young Black Americans ditched "Negro" for Black, "conked hair" for Afros, and called each other "Brothers and "Sisters. Guess what? Corporate America took heed and followed. This attempt at uplifting ourselves almost worked, until someone in our community thought of calling ourselves African American. Accepting this gave Black people an identity that seems to have come out of the marketing strategy of guilty White Liberal businesses.

In 2021, African American children continued to be the most neglected demographic in America. Black kids have not been a priority for the African American voter in any election since bussing; and that was for the wrong reason. Sitting beside White kids did not do anything for Black kids concerning learning. This neglect continued even during and after the historic election of the nation's first Black President. Throughout the Obama Administration, Black kids were stuck in cycles of poverty and crime, while drowning in blood from a murder and suicide epidemic. What makes it cruel and unusual is their mistreatment and abandonment is in the hands of their parents, who had a vote and chose to use it to vote against people they despise.

This book was completed in the year 2023. Since the election of the first African American President in 2008, there have been three presidential elections and 24 or more congressional, local, and state election cycles. African American Democrats did not risk a single vote for their children during that time. Nor did they give as much as a casual nod to the issues facing their children. I believe millions of Black lives would change overnight if African American Democrats so much as hinted they might vote differently the next time. Instead, African American voters are always complicit when the Democrat Party does things antithetical to Black kids learning and living.

The collateral damage from unearned loyalty to the Democrat Party has been visited on Black children like a plague. Today the demographics of Black children in America paints a picture of a people at odds with the God that delivered them.

- Homicide is the leading cause of death among Black youth
- 87% of Black kids are not proficient in reading and math
- Black babies have a higher low birth rate than any other group
- Black youth suicide deaths rate increasing faster than any group
- Black kids are three times more likely to be victims of child abuse
- Black youths are five times more likely to be murdered
- African Americans have murdered 350,000 Black Americans and aborted over 19 million Black babies since 1973

As previously stated, Black children are the only people the African American community will blame and hold responsible for their behavior. When bad things happen to our children, it is never the fault of the grown-ups who created these hellholes for Black kids to live in. On the other hand, when they are shot by the police, they are loved. Contrast the concern after a police shooting with the growing suicide rate among the Black kids they ignore and neglect.

After the latest suicide in my community, I talked with community adults. Everyone claimed the children were "hardheaded and disrespectful. They even claimed the Klan had hung them. These kids with documented cases of abuse were less loved than dope dealers who are killed by the police after poisoning Black children. Even White pedophiles receive more support than Black kids. We saw the proof of that during the Kyle Rittenhouse trial. Woke African Americans turned three White criminals into African American social justice warriors.

No issue says more about what is going on inside the Black community than the growing suicide rate among young Black kids. I live in a small town in the rural south. The Black population in our town and the surrounding communities is less than 1,000. In this small Black population, suicides outnumber murders among the young. There have been four suicides that I know of and no murders. When families with relatives living elsewhere are included, the suicide rate is more than double. Suicides by Black kids who are not loved are ignored, because the leading causes of suicides are child abuse and neglect at the hands of adults. Therefore, solutions to end the abuse are rejected by the adults. Instead of helping, the adults continue their calls for more abuse in the form of "whippings."

Choosing politics over religious values is the reason why Black demographics today look more like the result of a curse than the result of a lack of equal opportunity or racism. For more than half a century, the Black Left have continually discovered new ways to ignore the problems of Black youth and propagate the idea that our young are just violent or stupid and have no value. Today's young Black Americans, long removed from memories of Jim Crow, have adopted from their parents and grandparents the beliefs that Black people only feel pain when White people inflict it, that life only has value when a White person takes that life, and that Black people are owed something.

Larry Elder, a conservative radio personality, said the biggest problem that keeps African Americans from growing intellectually as a group is our refusal to accept a higher truth. He said that, if African American Democrats believe something, no amount of current information will change their minds. What Larry Elders described is cognitive dissonance, which psychologists define as *the state of having inconsistent thoughts, beliefs, or attitudes, especially relating to behavioral decisions and attitude change.*

I call it being Hebrew Slave stubborn. With no opposing voices in the Black community, there is no path to changing that attitude and helping Black children.

> *1 John 4:1-6. This is the spirit of the antichrist, which you have heard is coming and even now is already in the world.*

I cannot hold a conversation with an adult in the community or go on social media without someone saying something about how good God is. You may or may not have noticed that African Americans never vote with or support Conservative Christians. From the founding of the Republican Party to the civil rights movement, every racist and evil force Black Americans faced or were liberated from was led by

God-inspired people. And yet, they will not acknowledge them in prayer, deeds, or church. This is the behavior reserved for the "last days." Visit any family or community, and it will look like African Americans have been Raptured.

African American Christians vote with and support Atheists, Marxists, and a few other Anti-God groups. Yet 85% of African Americans say they are Christian. When the Biden Administration started supporting laws allowing people to pick their gender and implementing policies straight out of Revelations, African American Christian Democrats were on board. Furthermore, the verdict in the Kyle Rittenhouse trial showed which side African American Christians were on. An African American career criminal ran down and murdered Christians celebrating the birth of Christ. Because of their politics, Woke African American Christians took the side of the criminal.

The political divide in America is a mere skirmish compared to the Armageddon-like schism in the Black community. In one of his comedy sketches, Chris Rock joked about a "civil war" in the Black community. Right now, it is mother against father, father against son, gang wars, and rumors of more gang wars. The only thing missing is a plague of locusts. If one speaks outside the community about the causes of the condition, Woke African Americans will attack you, using hundreds of years of Black oppression as a shield. When they attack you, they claim to be the victim. If you are White, they will sell their souls to the government, corporate America, or Big Tech to silence or fire you. If you live in the community, you will be attacked, maybe killed. And if your business depends on their dollars, you will be boycotted, kicked off the TV, looted, and your property burned.

The people causing the divide are the same kind of people who are the subject of this book. Throughout this book, I write about the racism and racist violence African Americans have covered up and participated in, on behalf of the people they claim are oppressing them. Ingratitude has made Black America the worst Hell a Black child can be born into if they get past the abortionist and make it through the birth canal.

I am old enough to remember better times. It was not always like it is today, with everything being racist. There is a new kind of African American racism and hate, which began long after the Black Muslims stopped, talking of "White Devils." This rejuvenated racism and hatred began with the election of Barack Obama and was practiced throughout the administration of Donald Trump. With the help of educated Democrat White women, the same forces that created the Ku Klux Klan turned African American Democrats into a hate group and called it equity. In 2021 with racism on a ventilator, Woke African Americans and White Progressives started claiming names, statues, climate, roads, and bridges were racist.

All the marching and bus rides for voting rights had finally paid off. Once Obama was in office, everything was seen as being about race. This strategy was alright with Obama, because he did not want to go with a Black agenda. Instead, Obama stoked division. Rather than seeing the country had taken a giant leap towards a more perfect union, Woke African Americans following President Obama acted as if he was a God and threatened elected African Americans if they didn't support Obama's race-baiting agenda.

One cannot become a hate-filled racist without someone to hate. The hate came for permanent residency with the election of Donald J Trump. Maybe I should say the learned hate came to stay with the election of Donald Trump. African American Democrats considered Trump's tweets worse than the history of Jim Crow.

If someone doubts it's taught hatred, compare Woke African Americans and the Ku Klux Klan, or ask a hardcore racist Klansmen why they hate Martin Luther King. After you ask the racist/Klansman, turn and ask African American Democrats why they hate Donald Trump; both would give the same answer, just worded differently. You might hear something like; he's a liar, a rapist, a communist or, a racist. It is hatred, not politics when people choose to let their children die rather than accept help from a person they hate. Like the poor Whites who fought a five-year war over slaves they were never going to own, Democrats got African Americans to make the same kind of sacrifice.

I had to fight racism before realizing it was not the root cause of Black people's problems. The one thing African Americans are not allowed to know is that we have overcome. In the absence of that knowledge, the racism we experienced and fought to end has been replaced by something more evil, more injurious, more ruinous, and even more tragic than slavery or Jim Crow. What is coming is told to us in *1 John 4:1-6: This is the spirit of the antichrist, which you have heard is coming and even now is already in the world.*

As the Bible promised, this evil is here and manifested in a leadership class of people willing to apply it to the least of us. Even with thousands of years of warnings, we will still line up for 6 6 6.

The Caste System

From the beginning of this book, I proved the existence of two separate and unequal Black Americas. I make this distinction because the Woke African American majority has made it clear there are two Black Americas. On behalf of Conservatives, I accept this arrangement because any form of woke slavery is unacceptable as a condition for freethinking people.

Living separate and unequal lives does not mean African Americans will not treat the color Black like a franchise they own. When a Black Conservative criticizes the behavior of African American Democrats individually or as a group, they will claim you hate your "own" race, or you hate Black people. Those of us who do not learn to obey lose their color franchise. To help enforce the rules, a curse in the form of a Black Ruling Class came to prominence. This group, who stood by OJ while throwing Cosby to the wolves, will view my book as an attack on the Black race. They will then call their White Liberal masters and sic them on me.

Most sane people would find it hard to believe that a brutal ruling class system exists among people who seem joined in a common struggle. Unlike most class systems, which are built on the wealth of generations, this caste system is built on the statistics of the poor, the Black working-class, historical racism, and made-to-order bigotry. To fill their coffers and lust for power, poor and working-class Black people are milked daily like herds of Guernsey cattle for their misery statistics.

The African American Ruling Class, nurtured in the protective bosom of the Democrat Party and tucked in the pocket of Corporate America, has turned civil rights into silver and gold rights. The conditions created under this class system are manufactured out of lies and the parasitic needs of corrupt churches, politicians, and nonprofit organizations. In Black America today, every baby born into poverty and every criminal from that birth is fathered by an industry dependent on grievance and ripe for political and economic exploitation. To protect their interests, the press, the civil rights industry, and now lawyers like Ben Crump stalk Black males like a "hungry bear in Autumn", to use a line from a poem by Mary Oliver.

For the African American Ruling Class, life is good. Banked by the White Liberal billionaire class, the ruling class job is to keep large numbers of Black people misinformed and uneducated. This is in addition to keeping the masses on drugs, and believing they are the victims of systemic racism even if the racism happened 200 years ago. The civil rights organizations they control are still alive long after Jim Crow died. They benefit from high-paying jobs in political patronage mills like the EEOC, where they manufacture racism and create poverty. With the help of the Left, they created non-profit organizations that never address the needs of the poor and working class. For delivering the Black vote, the people they rape get to celebrate the First Black this or that.

With the Black masses under their control, the African American Ruling Class has control of a disposable income that is larger than two-thirds of the world's countries Gross National Product. This income is steered into the bank accounts of Corporate America. The people under the control of the leadership class have so much political power they can even elect a senile old man as President. Jim Clyburn proved that in 2020 when Woke African Americans went to the polls in record numbers to elect Biden and demanded nothing in return. Even when victimized and used, most African Americans are conditioned by the ruling class to blame the least threatening White person and too obey.

In one of Dr. Martin Luther King's Jr speeches, he uses the term "We as a people." I will argue that there is no "we" in Black America anymore. Under this class system, "we" are the leadership class and they are wearing iron boots. When they finish raping the Black race, there are only bones left to pick at.

To the ruling class, race trumps everything. The self-inflicted pain and suffering of Black people are not measured by the amount of blood spilled on sidewalks. Nor is pain and suffering measured by the number of children living in squalor or dying from hopelessness while hanging from the light fixture in their closet. Pain and suffering are measured by dollars based on how many Blacks have been shot by a White person. Even the tears of mothers with dead children shot by police are for sale, because Ben Crump is on speed dial.

In our culture, pain and suffering only happen to Black people in the form of racism. Self-inflicted wounds are never part of the problem or solution. The suffering of Black people under this class system, whether self-inflicted or during slavery, will always be treated like a commodity for sale. The only word most African Americans need to hear from the Ruling class is racism, and on hearing that word, they will behave as if they have come out of a Pavlovian laboratory.

Imagine that you live in Black America; then these are the unpleasant facts. There are more young people in the criminal justice system than in college; the leading cause of death among young Black people is murder; AIDS is now a black disease; and 70% of all children are born out of wedlock. I could name hundreds of Black issues. However, if it is not about racism or protecting the tribal leaders of the ruling class, there will be no outcry, and the D.A.A.M. (Democrat African American Majority) will not care.

The Virginia and California governor's races in 2021 proved exactly how laboratory racism had conditioned African Americans. In both races, to get out the Black vote, the African American Ruling Class came out in droves. They brought out Obama, the first African

American President. They also brought out Kamala Harris, the first woman of color to be Vice President, Corey Booker, a Black Senator, and a real live, self-aggrandizing female race hustler, Stacy Abrams, to campaign for Terry McAuliffe. They all knew not to appeal to African American voters to vote for better schools, safer streets, or anything to improve Black life. Given all the Black community's problems, they went straight to racism. For the first time, it did not work. Enough African Americans in Virginia became Black enough to reject exploitation and choose their children's future.

Most Americans are under no illusions about racism and its history. However, neither American History nor Black History record black-on-black violence as part of anyone's genocide. The victims under this caste system often exist as the victims of racism. However, compared to other atrocities, black class bigotry and the self-hate it has created belong in a history book alongside the likes of Mao, Stalin, and the Khmer Rouge. "We as a people" faced bloodthirsty mobs, vicious dogs, and governors with their "...lips dripping with the words of interposition and nullification" only to become slaves to Masters who look like us.

☐No history book, archive, or museum contains more evidence that an oppressive class system exists than Black History Month. Civil rights contributions by the victim class and Black Conservatives have been left entirely out of Black History Month by the Ruling Class.

As a factual matter, the civil rights movement was born out of an act of class bigotry. For instance, it is impossible to celebrate

Black History Month without recognizing members of the ruling class. However, nowhere in Black History will you find where Rosa Parks and 15-year-old Claudette Colvin each heard their calling on the same bus line. Finally, long after the death of Rosa Parks, in the year 2021 the Ruling Class started allowing Americans to hear about Claudette Colvin. Ms. Colvin was thus granted clemency by the leadership class who had robbed her of a place in history.

It was Ms. Colvin's calling that led to the Supreme Court ruling that ended segregation on the Montgomery bus line Rosa Parks made her stand on. Unlike Mrs. Parks, who became an icon, Ms. Colvin's contributions were not recognized by as much as an asterisk on a Black History Month calendar. Because of Ms. Colvin's class status, her history was also raped, and the crime and the crime against her ignored.

In an article from the Washington Post titled: "The Ladies Before Rosa." Staff Writer Paul Hendrickson's unintended confirmation of an African American class system also shows the bigotry that exists in the press. Hendrickson described the two women this way:

While one was a highly emotional 11th grader about whom there were unsavory stories and who lived in a house that didn't have an indoor toilet, the other, Mrs. Parks – as so much of Montgomery respectfully thought of her – was a small, modest, ascetic-looking wholly untainted women and civic activist and youth leader: a perfect and righteous symbol for igniting not just a yearlong boycott but an entire movement. "They didn't want me because of where I lived and what my parents' background was."

Suffering from the pains of rejection and being ostracized by her race, Ms. Colvin thought about committing suicide as a way to deal with the rejection. Place this act of bigotry in context with Jesus Christ's teachings and the Holy Bible's promise that the meek shall inherit the earth. It's no wonder the path the civil rights movement took led many Black people into abject poverty and created a millionaire leadership class to rule over the Black race.

Maintaining the class system does not allow the poor and working class to become heroes. To be recognized for their contributions, people like Ms. Colvin must be rescued or assisted by members of the class system. Even the African American masses themselves go along with discriminating against their class. It is clear from the article that Ms. Colvin was unwanted as an icon.

Toya Graham faced the same treatment as "The Women Before Rosa…" During the Baltimore Riots over the death of Freddie Gray, Toya Graham made national news when she dragged her son from the streets after she recognized him under a mask, throwing rocks at the police. Ms. Graham was trying to save her son's life when she was slapped with the "stay in your place" backhand.

Instead of welcoming her, the African American community did to her exactly what they had done to Claudette Colvin for refusing to give up her seat before Rosa Parks. I knew from the moment I saw Ms. Graham that the entire African American community would ostracize her. There would be no reality TV show, book deal, speaking engagements, or GoFundMe for Toya. Even her family turned on her. The Washington Post reported that her brother, Robert Graham became furious that the rest of the family did not get the recognition they deserved. The article goes on to say that the family has "splintered."

****

Once it became known that she was from the poor and working-class, she too would be shunned like Clarence Thomas and other Black Conservatives who are shunned for their politics. The nail in the coffin for Toya Graham came when she appeared on Fox News. That became the pretext to ruin her. It was also the wink, nod, and gun from the African American Ruling Class to the mainstream media and the White Liberal community not to make her a hero. I cannot recall ever seeing, hearing, or reading about her in the African American media.

The progressives in the mainstream media had received their signal from the ruling class. Once the Washington Post ran a story about Toya Graham, she was on her way to being beaten down as recorded by the press. The headline read, "What happened to the 'hero mom' of Baltimore's riots?" The online article begins with a picture of her in her bedclothes standing outside her home. During the interview, she showed the reporter her eviction notice. Ms. Graham also stated she was earning just $10.00 an hour. The article did not mention why the Black community did not embrace her as they had Freddy Graves, but we know why.

In a May 4, 2015, article by Wendi C. Thomas and titled, "Baltimore doesn't need more mothers like Toya Graham," Wendi Thomas unleashed a scathing attack on Ms. Graham and mothers who wants to save their sons. This attack brings to reality the class system that exist within the Black culture. In a city run by the Black Ruling Class Wendi Thomas writes: "Better parenting won't make the Baltimore police department follow its own policies. Black mothers are expected to sacrifice their sons because African Americans elected official do not have the will to fire police officers and stand up to unions

Black History Month is not supposed to be about Selective Black History. For example, my cousin bet me that Lincoln owned slaves. At least ten other people joined the conversation and agreed with him. When I proved they were wrong, they all used the "White Man wrote the book" excuse. In addition to that, not one of those who disagreed would accept that the Democrat Party created the KKK and fought to keep slavery. Black History Month has been around for almost 100 years, and all it has done is erase the Democrats' history of oppressing the Black race. For nearly 100 years, Black History Month has been in the wrong hands and is now a tool to promote Black classism and victimization. Black Republicans, in particular, are rejected outright or mentioned by name with no reference to the party.

Black History Month is not alone in spreading this form of oppression. Black Conservatives' critical appraisals of work by black filmmakers, such as Spike Lee, note how Lee and other directors avoid dramatizations of classism within the black community and how it affects Black people. The role the Black media plays in the making of the two Black Americas is evident in the rebirth of black sitcoms. Every black show on network Black TV today is about Black Liberal professionals. Shows like "Amos and Andy" are banned as stereotypes. Gone are shows centering around the Black poor and working class. "Sanford and Son," a show about a father and son in the junk business is confined to nostalgia TV. "Good Times," a show about the Evans family, a black family, complete with a father struggling while living in the projects, has gone to the land of reruns. However, before they canceled the show, they removed the father from his home. The results of what Hollywood Liberals did to the Evans family can be seen in the statistics of Black people. Today, too many black families look like not-so-good times, with single women heading most Black households.

"I thought the kids were bad until I saw the parents." This charge by Bill Cosby, although valid, is that of a wealthy actor and philanthropist far removed from his observation. Although he was in the ballpark, he only had enough information to swing at the truth. However, his comment foretells dire consequences for a race that has grown stubborn and far too comfortable being hit in the head with a two-by-four before taking preventative measures. Mr. Cosby's statement also violated the Black Code of Silence. Once again, the ruling class gave the wink and nod to White Progressives, and Bill Cosby was carted off to jail with their blessings.

In 2023, morgues, prisons, and welfare rolls are still overflowing with Black kids. Their future is so uncertain that a pregnancy in their ranks should be called a "miscarriage of justice." They are on the verge of self-annihilation, and this wealthy actor/comedian and philanthropist knew this and said it aloud. Bill Cosby knew and said that the problems of Black children are as close as the adults sitting in their living room. Mr. Cosby suggests it is reasonable to assume that these children got their self-destructive behavior from their parents alone. Even Bill Cosby could not understand or explain that the children and their parents' self-destructive behaviors were part and parcel of something ordered by the African American Ruling Class.

In making this charge, I do not want to paint with too wide or too narrow a brush. Mr. Cosby's judgment grew out of his observation from an ivory perch. He would later learn that telling the truth about Black America is hazardous to your health and freedom. When White Liberals wanted a Black trophy for their #MeToo Movement, the African American Ruling Class handed him over. Imagine that. One of Black America's iconic members is brought before Caesar amidst the silence of the masses of African Americans who supported OJ and later gave their support to the White pedophile who Kyle Rittenhouse shot.

1 Peter 3:14 But even if you should suffer for what is right, you are blessed. "Do not fear their threats; do not be frightened."

Until I got out of my place, I had no idea the Black community had a brutal caste system long after the Black Power Movement ended. I mentioned this before. In this system, your class status and voter registration determine your position in the culture, and whether or not you can speak on specific issues or be recognized for good deeds. Trying to do good or what is right, or even challenging the status quo outside one's status generates even more hate than siding with Trump.

Bobby Person and I became victims of the caste system when we sued a sitting Democrat Governor and his African Americans appointees. By doing so, we faced a dual system of bigotry, even though Bobby is a hardcore Democrat. While Bobby and I fought racists and Klansmen at the prison and the courts, we were also fighting politicians, civil rights organizations, the press, and the Black community who were protecting the racists. Just like Jesus returning to his hometown, they made us feel unwelcome and unwanted in our hometown, in our families, and within our very own race.

Bobby and I held many press conferences, but the interviews never advanced our cause. Every time we did a press conference or talk show, the press would edit out anything about the African Americans in charge. To remedy that, I asked Bobby Person and Hilton Dunlap to join me and create a radio program to tell our own story. We paid for the program out of our pockets and later with Z.

Smith Reynolds grants. In the beginning, the program was called Radio Activist Monitoring Black and Racist Organizations (R.A.M.B.R.O.). Later, we changed the name to Voices for Justice. Our work in the community won the Nancy Susan Reynolds Award. I would find out that being a Conservative leads to you being ostracized. Bobby and Hilton were invited to attend and receive the award at the ceremony. I was left out.

With the program came the hate from the Black community, and I caught the worse of it. I lived in the predominately Black town of Taylortown with its ruthless ruling class and gullible sycophants who enforced the rules and propped up its ruling class. Late in the night, people would call my house and say they "wished" the Klan would kill my children and me.

****

Before leaving Taylortown for Virginia, I was President of the Concerned Citizens of Taylortown. Our group sued the All-Black town council because they were corrupt and treated residents as subjects. The Concerned Citizens decided that Derrick and I should run in the election. We were unopposed up to the day they started counting votes. When they finished counting, two write-ins won. They didn't know how their names had been included, so they refused to take the seat. Rather than choose us, they appointed a minister and former janitor, Cobie Ransom, who could barely read. I am sure he was a great janitor, because the post office had a big picture of him on the wall with the caption: "man with the broom."

Election night turned out to be a horror. When I arrived home, I found out my girlfriend (who would later be my wife) had taken "my" children to her mother's house in a community named Zion Grove. I got into my car and drove to Zion Grove to get the kids. On the day of the election, my neighbor, Leon Ransom's home was robbed, and his guns stolen. I found out that my niece was involved, and I made her get the weapons and bring them to me. Those weapons were in the car when I arrived in Zion Grove. I picked up the guns to move them, one of the guns fired and hit my mother-in-law's house. I went in to apologize, but my mother-in-law had already called the police. She did not file charges; however, the sheriff's department did.

I was arrested and taken to the county jail. With this arrest, the ruling class had finally broken me. I felt so hopeless, I decided to just stay in jail. Several days passed, and I had not eaten. That night a White jailer came to my cell. He told me that he and other officers knew I was being railroaded and I needed to leave because I did not belong in jail. The jailer said that Superintendent Marion had come to the jail and talked to the sheriff about sending me to the mental hospital because I was not eating. The jailer told me that he and other officers would pay my bail and buy me steaks or anything I wanted to eat. The jailer also told me I should not let the DOC win. I called someone and went home.

I could not find decent work in Moore County, so I left Taylortown for Alexandria, Virginia. When my marriage ended, I decided to move back into a home I owned in Taylortown. I should have known the hate I had left 15 years earlier would be awaiting my return. Before I moved back, the African American Mayor of Taylortown, Ulysses Barrett, sent me a letter condemning my home. He then hired a company to bury it on-site and placed a $500 lien on the property. After some protest, the county ordered him to dig up the house because burying a house was illegal. So the Mayor dug up my home, and the cost of digging it up was added to the lien on the property.

Now I had no home in Taylortown, and Taylortown's election

was near. I wrote a letter to the Moore County Board of Election explaining that I lived in Vass and wanted to remain a resident of Taylortown. I asked if I could run in the upcoming town election. They told me yes, so I did. Shortly after this, an African American woman named Katherine Brown filed a complaint. I had to appear before the Moore County Board of Election. Ansol Graham, another African American ruling class member, took away my voting rights.

During the hearing, Mr. Graham was disrespectful and rude, and he constantly interrupted when I questioned Mrs. Brown during the hearing. At the time, I did not know that Mr. Graham was a friend of Jesse Fuller, a fellow teacher and Taylortown town council member I had sued on behalf of the Concerned Citizens of Taylortown. That was one of the reasons Mr. Graham was so unprofessional and hateful. I would learn a little later from a cousin that Ansol Graham, a former teacher at Pinecrest High School, had quite a reputation with female students. My niece told me that Ansol Graham had impregnated my cousin while she was a student at Pinecrest High School. I could say more, but family members could get hurt.

Whether it is a peaceful protest march or a violent riot, it becomes a product repurposed by the Left and designed to benefit members of the African American Ruling Class. Most Americans are aware of the violence and destruction that followed the death of George Floyd. In most cases involving police shootings of Black males like George Floyd, the prayers that were absent and needed when he was alive become the answer to their deaths.

Like all similar deaths, Floyd's death highlights how well trained the African Americans masses are. Any deaths caused by Whites or a not guilty verdict justify the self-defeating behavior of burning down the community, robbing, looting, and burning stores that will never return, with their jobs and fresh food. It is also like winning the Powerball for the families of these victims and their lawyers. However, the biggest beneficiaries and those pulling the strings are people like Vice President Kamala Harris, who went on a bail fundraising spree. That act alone points in the direction of those who are benefiting. She became our first pandering Black Vice President.

On the other hand, had Floyd died from his excesses or a bullet from the street, like most of the other Black men who are killed, the elites of the ruling class and the community would have shunned him. They would have stepped over his dead body, walked over to a Popeye's, and shot each other over a chicken sandwich. Furthermore, they would cover for their leaders as they did for Sharpton and Marion Berry. Floyd being dead with a White man to blame is not a tragedy to them. It is revenue; it is votes; it is high-paying jobs, TV shows, a path to citizenship, climate change, voter reform and being transgender. When tragedies like this happen, it is never a teaching moment or a lightbulb moment. It is never a time to demand better schools or address issues in the Black community. It is always an opportunity to exploit and exact vengeance.

Consider the Klan rape and murder of Joyce Sinclair I mentioned earlier. Almost 35 years have passed since the racist murder of Joyce Sinclair and other Black and Native Americans in Robeson County, NC. There has not been a single call for God to heap vengeance on her rapist and killer or even capture the killer. African Americans know to take their cue from the Ruling Class members through their proxies in the media. Woke African Americans are conditioned to know when the media does not report a particular murder, rape, or racist act; they know without being told an African American or Democrat is involved, and they are to stay silent and obey.

Following a well-defined narrative, People like Akilah P. Davis, a reporter for WTVD, will show you their bigotry and disdain for poor and working-class Black people when they believe the people beneath them are not a threat or on a mission from God. While I was on Facebook, I responded directly to a Facebook post of Ms. Davis about abuses at the EEOC. I emailed her about the millions of complaints of race, sex, and other forms of discrimination filed with the EEOC. I told her that, even though the government has admitted the EEOC violated victims' rights, most African Americans like herself follow the narrative set by the Liberal media and the corporate oligarchs.

From: Jimmy Pratt <shemdiz@yahoo.com>
Sent: Sunday, April 18, 2021, 9:34:49 AM
To: Davis, Akilah P. <Akilah.P.Davis@abc.com>
Subject: Corona Racism
OPEN LETTER TO: Akilah P Davis

I read your Facebook post citing the CDC declaration that racism is a public health issue. It is odd, even tragic how quickly you in the professional class embrace victimization and spread it with the precision of a deadly virus. They even gave you a title, Race and Culture Reporter, how nice. However, I am a little puzzled because the EEOC posted over 2 million charges of race and sex discrimination and I've never seen a protest or a news story about it. How can someone be suffering from mental anguish brought on by racism and I can't find anywhere on their Facebook page or the news where they were a victim or know a victim? Must be that Stockholm Syndrome thing. Since they have no racism to cite, I must assume it's racism by proxy caused by the police shootings of African Americans they don't know. Better yet maybe it was bought on by the actual race victims cited in these EEOC Charge Statistics. It has to be traumatic working side by side with racism victims of workplace racism that the GAO says are being abused by a government agency and not seeing anything. You know; I actually put the EEOC statistics on my Facebook page and my friends saw a police shooting and a White man confronting a Black teen walking in the neighborhood.

I'm not looking forward to a reply because I've long grown use to when pigs fly and Hell freezing over!

On Sunday, April 18, 2021, 09:38:38 AM EDT, Davis, Akilah P. <akilah.p.davis@abc.com> wrote:

It's always funny when the boldness of blind ignorance makes its way to your inbox. Just so you know, when nimwits like you email reporters, we don't read them. Stop wasting your time, buddy. I get it – you're lonely and have no life. Please find something better to do with your time. And kindly, stay off my Facebook page.

From: Jimmy Pratt <shemdiz@yahoo.com>
Sent: Sunday, April 18, 2021, 9:34:49 AM
To: Davis, Akilah P. <Akilah.P.Davis@abc.com>
Subject: Corona Racism

The reporter, Akilah P. Davis, who is attacking me in the above email, used her ruling class member's card. The worst thing about this ethnic caste system is that the subjects are the victims and the enforcers. Facebook has made it possible for me to mine the hate people like me face daily. I'm sure Americans have heard the racial slurs aimed at people like Supreme Court Justice Clarence Thomas, Dr. Ben Carson, and Senator Tim Scott. Those who have done the least to advance the Black race are even more threatening and intimidating at a family or social gathering and social media. They should know by now; Black Conservatives know God, and we believe God did not give us the spirit of fear.

Hypocrisy and Duplicity

Looking back through African Americans' history of suppressing speech, mandating behavior, and shackling down co-operation, it is easy to see that Black America was the laboratory for what is playing out in America today. The Left learned exactly how to force people to comply and like it from that laboratory.

Forcing obedience has been a mission of Democrats since Johnson said he would have N*****s voting Democrat for the next 100 years. If you are a card-carrying Democrat in the African American community, you are the reason boys can be girls and bridges are racist. So, if you accept being obedient, hate-filled, ostracized, and silenced, you are the people President Johnson predicted African Americans would become. Maybe you can't change because there is about 47 years left for the Johnson prediction.

Look closely at any race riot. The riots in Portland and other places were not incited by acts of racism or the actions of racists or the police. The riots were instigated by the same people who called the riots "mostly peaceful..." When you look at any riot, one fact will become clear; African Americans never riot when the victim is a woman or when it's Black on Black. The rioting over the death of Breonna Taylor was an extension of George Floyd. They just threw her in to make it look like they cared. Likewise, the same duplicity is at work when a Black police officer in Memphis killed Tyre Nichols. Somehow, those African American police officers became White Supremacist... When the victim is a Black male, and the other person is White, Woke African Americans do not wait for evidence. It's judgment day immediately. No evidence of a crime is needed when the requirements of the narratives are met.

The duplicity does not stop at police shootings. I know adults who do not parent their children. They will spend all year yelling at the child about being lazy, using drugs, or any other kind of misbehaving. When the child gets in trouble, they blame White people.

The same duplicity and hypocrisy are at work in the sworn complaints of approximately 70,000 Black victims of workplace discrimination. The press and the civil rights community never see wrong. These victims have been languishing at the EEOC for years, waiting for a determination from an Administrative Judge. African Americans work side by side, eight hours a day, 40 hours a week with these race victims and the White people they call racist. Yet they never report seeing any racism. However, on social media and in the press, they claim racism is systemic. They all claim racism is everywhere. However, a researcher cannot find 20 friends and relatives of Bobby Person and me who can tell you anything about the racism he and I faced at the Moore County Prison. I guess they cannot support fighting racism when that support gets in the way of their racial hypocrisy.

I often say God could come to America early in the morning and change the heart of every White racist. Before the six o'clock news air, Al Sharpton would be protesting racism, and most African Americans would support him. The truth is that African American Democrats will never give up racism as a tool to shake down businesses and bully White people into guilt. Today in America, making a racist charge is more valuable than a college degree or a winning lottery ticket.

Another case to keep in mind when pointing out hypocrisy is the case that I mentioned earlier: Bobby Person VS. Carolina Knights of the KKK. The hate, jealousy, and ostracism against Bobby are noticeable when accolades on his birthday, Veteran's Day, and Father's Day are contrasted with Black History Month. Family and friends have no problem showing love and support on days outside Black History Month. For birthdays on Facebook, Bobby received hundreds of likes and comments. On the other hand, when it's Black History Month, family and friends shun Bobby's landmark lawsuit against the Klan as if it were a dirty COVID mask. Considering Bobby Person's landmark victory over the most prominent and fastest growing Klan group in America, one would think there would be a little gratitude expressed in the entire month for which we celebrate Black History. Woke African Americans cut Bobby no slack, and, as I previously said, he is a Democrat.

Our former classmates followed the examples of Facebook friends and relatives. Before every class reunion, they would send letters asking classmates to send in any good work they had done to be honored. Bobby sent in a newspaper clipping about his victory over the Klan. The reunion committee decided not to give an award for that year.

The same hypocrisy happens every year when Black History Month rolls around. Family and friends will not mention our victory over the Klan or our successful fight to end discrimination in hiring procedures at the Moore County Prison. In my case, I was called a Tom or sellout, sometimes by both friends and relatives with no civil rights record. When I show them my civil rights record, they dismiss it as having been a long time ago. In that same argument about racism "a long time ago," they will dredge up things that happened during slavery. Others in chat groups on Facebook even claimed that I stole Jimmy Pratt's story. However, had the Klan killed us, there would be memes all over social media all year round.

Bobby Person and I are not the only ones attacked for either fighting racism or simply trying to help Black people. Singer Chrisette Michele's singing career was effectively ended when she sang at President Trump's Inauguration. The very people who silenced that beautiful voice voted for, Senator Robert Byrd a former Grand Dragon of the Ku Klux Klan, Ralph Northam a governor in blackface, and George Wallace a governor who stood in the schoolhouse doorway to block black kids from entering.

When a person in the Black community do something to help the community, and there's a conflict with the political status quo, that person is expendable. Two of the most notable people who ran into this double standard were Tavis Smiley and Cornel West. Together with Al Sharpton, they authored *The State of the Black Union*. This report was supposed to be laid by on the desk of the "next" President regardless of party, color. When that President became Barack Obama, Woke African American Democrats destroyed Tavis Smiley and Cornell West for keeping their promise to lay the report on Obama's desk. Out of the blue, there came sex charges against Tavis Smiley. The community labeled him an Uncle Tom. PBS and Urban Radio kicked him off the air. By contrast, Al

Sharpton, who turned on Smiley and West, was rewarded with a TV show, and President Obama crowned him Czar of the Black race.

FACT! The majority of African Americans in the Black community either cover up or participate in the racism they claim to be fighting. Getting and keeping control of the racial narrative is more about profit than liberation. Unlike King and Malcolm X, civil rights leaders today become millionaires and expect to be treated that way. Contrast Al Sharpton flying to a protest on a private jet with Dr. King and others who walked from Selma to Montgomery in their own blood. Also, consider Al Sharpton at a protest rally selfishly demanding police protection from the very police he wanted to be defunded.

Trying to keep up with a race of people whose Christian values change each election cycle is like chauffeuring Virgil through Hell in Dante's Inferno. Because you share the same race, you have to ride along with some things. After all the sacrifices, the Woke Christians who Dr. King, Malcolm X, Medgar Evers, and others gave their lives for adopted the same hate that killed these great people. I have seen that hate on display many times. For example, as soon as the jury was empaneled in the trial of Derek Chauvin for the murder of George Floyd, so-called Christians started bending scriptures and prayers into tools of vengeance and hate. They called on God to let them be judges and jury – and for God to let not his will be done but theirs.

In the absence of a meme that tells Woke African Americans what to think and do, most of them turn to God and Facebook to push their hate agenda. Below are a couple of Facebook posts after the George Floyd verdict.

GUILTY THANK YOU, GOD. IT'S A NEW DAY.

*TB GOD IS GOOD **LC** Yyeessss!! JM Bout time JP Yes BB O yes **AD** 🙌 VC C Yes JS God is Good RM Amen Peterson Yes! CC It is about time TR Amen!*

It was not enough that a jury found former Minnesota officer Derek Chauvin guilty on all counts. On that same day, a 16-year-old Black girl was shot and killed by a White police officer while trying to kill another Black girl. In an attempt to show solidarity with the least among us, LeBron James, a Black multi-millionaire basketball player, doxed the officer. African American Democrats from Joy Reid to friends on my Facebook page were outraged that the police officer had stopped a Black-on-Black killing. The shooting blew apart their White on Black narrative and exposed the hypocrisy that makes everything racial. The Black-on-black carnage that was in the making, between the girls, was "all good" until the racial component was blown apart by good intentions. In that same week, a 13-year-old Black girl stabbed to death another Black girl, and those outraged people were happy to stack her dead body on top of all the others they ignored.

Hypocrisy in the Black community has become deadlier than the COVID Virus and as contagious. Hypocrisy is as necessary as air for those in our community whose activities depend on it. It is the reason why Black people who they cannot control are called Uncle

Toms and White Supremacists by people who vote strictly for the people who enslaved the Black race

This is the same type of hypocrisy coupled with envy that killed Malcolm X. When Malcolm X was released from prison. Malcolm knew that the Black race needed to respect themselves before demanding others respect them. Eventually, Malcolm X ran into the hypocrisy and duplicity that claimed him, his wife, and some of his children and grandchildren. It saddens me that Malcolm's life ended in the hands of the people he was trying to save. It was too late when Malcolm learned that you cannot save people who don't know they need saving. And you cannot save the kind of people God left in the desert to die off.

As I previously stated, African Americans' demands for help ended with the election of President Obama. They are now the people Dr. King described: *One is a force of complacency, made up in part of Negroes who, as a result of long years of oppression, are so drained of self-respect and a sense of "somebodiness" that they have adjusted to segregation.*

When the Opposing Forces Dr. King spoke of dreamed up the 1619 project, Critical Race Theory, and Black Lives Matter, it was not to remove the last vestige of racism in America. These movements came to erase memories of Black men, women, and children who stood like giants and warriors sweeping away injustice as they marched, fought, and died. Their crusade created an arts renaissance, a Civil Rights movement, and a Black Power movement. These movements gave ownership to Black people that included a

Black man in the White House. While others were sacrificing, the people drained of self-respect prove Dr. King's thesis true. These same people are destroying the Black family and demanding resegregation. They are not to be judged by the content of their character.

I have always believed hypocrisy in the abstract was confined to the acts of individuals and even small groups. However, when almost an entire race of people are hypocrites, they follow a well-planned scheme. In the words of Carter Woodson, they do not have to be told what to think and say:

> *"If you can control a man's thinking you do not have to worry about his action. When you determine what a man shall think you do not have to concern yourself about what he will do. If you make a man feel that he is inferior, you do not have to compel him to accept an inferior status, for he will seek it himself. If you make a man think that he is justly an outcast, you do not have to order him to the back door. He will go without being told; and if there is no back door, his very nature will demand one."*
>
> – Carter Godwin Woodson, *The Mis-Education of the Negro*

As of December 2021, Carter Woodson's observation is playing out as if we were sitting in a multiplex. Every African American Democrat knows without being told not to say anything about Hunter Biden or the $450,000 offered to immigrants. And they know to go vote and ask for nothing in return. As we awaited the verdict in the Kyle Rittenhouse trial, African Americans knew to take the side of the criminals and ignore all the evidence. Had Trump won the election, millions of Woke African Americans would be dead of

COVID. They would not have taken the same vaccine under Trump they are taking under Biden.

Ask an African American Democrat to name just one Black issue they voted for or support. They will say things like Obamacare or the stimulus given out by President Biden. Others would label me with a slur and ask what the Republicans have done. Others would skip the subject or claim they are too intelligent to talk to people they believe to be intellectually inferior. Like the example below, Facebook friends can't and won't discuss life and death issues like poverty, Black on Black violence, or the evening news. And yet, they claim to have every answer to everything Black.

Since returning from Vietnam, I joined and worked with many civil rights groups and grass roots organizations. I learned from these outings that civil rights groups were little more than PACs for the Democrat Party. I learned through this association that trying to address a Black issue that the Left wants to exploit and mine for its racial value is almost impossible. As racism dies, those who profit from it create more oppression and injustice in the name of racism. By their nature, the majority of African Americans will go along with it.

Going Postal, Alexandria, VA Post Office

While I was fighting Simon Banks, employees from the Alexandria Post Office began contacting me for help. A Black supervisor named Tracy Wade had been accused of attacking at least one male worker and sexually assaulting female postal workers in the Alexandria Post Office. In addition to that, women were being forced to sleep with supervisors to keep their jobs or get promoted. Those charges are contained in letters and petitions sent to me and shared with civil rights groups, women groups, and members of congress.

All of these assaults took place after a postal worker had gone on a killing spree, creating the phrase, "going postal." I could only get a small newspaper, the Mount Vernon Gazette, to report it. Additional letters and a chronological list of assaults are in the index, along with a copy of my complaint to the Justice Department about inmate abuse and racism

The complaints were mailed out at the time when postal workers were killing people across the country due to mistreatment. Despite the carnage, no one investigated the sexual assaults, racism, and other abuses in post offices that led to the killing spree. These massacres represent just how hard it is to get help with a problem of discrimination, sexual abuse, or racism from government agencies, the press, and civil rights groups when the victims are profiled.

Jesse Jackson founder of PUSH/Rainbow had an office in DC that agreed to help. The director told me to document my complaint in writing and call them back. When I called back, the receptionist asked my name and put me on hold. She came back to the phone and told me the director was not in. I hung up and called back immediately. When the receptionist asked my name, I pretended to be a reporter. When the director picked up the phone, I said, "I thought you were not in." That was the end of PUSH's help.

****

A terror campaign was happening inside the U.S. post office in Alexandria, VA, and no one cared. Below is a list of postal shootings across the country. Following that are letters, a petition, and a chronological list of assaults postal workers complained about in one post office in Alexandria, Virginia.

I also sent copies of these documents to the Alexandria Human Rights Office. Once they found out an African American was the source of the complaints, no one helped. Unaddressed issues like the ones in the Alexandria post office were the kind that led to the following:

On August 20, 1986, in Edmond, Oklahoma, postal worker Patrick Sherrill chased and killed 14 co-workers and injured more before committing suicide. The following is a list of murders by postal workers that followed the Oklahoma massacre:

136

December 14, 1988, New Orleans, Louisiana: Warren Murphy entered into the New Orleans, Louisiana, postal facility with a 12-gauge shotgun hidden under his clothing. Later, during his work shift, after an incident with a supervisor, he reportedly went to the men's room and came out brandishing the shotgun. He then fatally shot his supervisor in the face. The fired shot reportedly wounded two other employees. After the shooting, he held his ex-girlfriend hostage. Later, two FBI SWAT agents were reportedly wounded upon finding Warren Murphy in a supervisor's office. He eventually surrendered to the agents.

August 10, 1989, Escondido, California: John Merlin Taylor killed his wife, then two colleagues, and himself at Orange Glen post office.

October 10, 1991: Ex-postal worker Joseph M. Harris killed his ex-supervisor and her boyfriend at their home in Wayne, New Jersey, then killed two former colleagues as they arrived at the Ridgewood, New Jersey post office where they all previously worked. According to "Today in Rotten History," Harris was initially armed with an Uzi, grenades, and "samurai sword" and was later arrested after a 41½ -hour standoff with police, garbed in a ninja's outfit and gas mask. He was convicted of murder and sentenced to death.

November 14, 1991, Royal Oak, Michigan: Fired postal worker Thomas McIlvaine killed four, and wounded five, before killing himself.

June 3, 1992, Citrus Heights, California: Roy Barnes, a 60-year-old employee, went to the workroom floor at the Citrus Heights post office, armed with a .22 caliber pistol, and fatally shot himself in the heart in front of his coworkers.

May 6, 1993, Dearborn, Michigan: Postal worker Larry Jason killed one, wounded three, then killed himself at a post office garage.

May 6, 1993, Dana Point, California: Mark Richard Hilbun, a former postal employee, killed his mother and her dog in their home. He then made his way to the post facility where he used to work and shot two postal workers, killing one and injuring the other. He continued the three-day rampage injuring multiple other people. The incident occurred after he had been dismissed for stalking another co-worker.

May 4, 1994, Pittsburgh, Pennsylvania: Postal employee James A. Paulano was accidentally killed in a drive-by shooting.

March 21, 1995, Montclair, New Jersey: Christopher Green, a former postal employee, killed four people (including two employees) and wounded a fifth at the Fairfield Street branch post office. While this is a postal killing, the primary motivation appears to have been debt payment, and there was no indication that the former employee was mentally disturbed as a result of his former postal work.

July 10, 1995, City of Industry, California: Bruce Clark, current employee and a postal clerk with 25 years employment with the USPS, subsequent to an argument, punched his supervisor in the back of the head at the City of Industry, California, mail processing center and left the work area. About ten minutes later, he returned to the work area with a brown paper bag in his hand. Upon being asked by his supervisor what was in the bag, he reportedly pulled out a .38 revolver and fired at close range; he fatally shot the supervisor twice, once in the upper body and once in the face. Two employees reportedly took the gun away from Clark and held him until police arrived. Seventy-five postal employees reportedly witnessed the shooting.

December 19, 1996, Las Vegas, Nevada: Former employee Charles Jennings went to the parking lot at the Las Vegas, Nevada, postal facility and shot and killed a labor relations specialist. Mr. Jennings reportedly indicated in his statement to investigators that the labor relations specialist struggled to take the gun away from him and was shot in the process.

September 2, 1997, Miami Beach, Florida: 21-year postal employee Jesus Antonio Tamayo shot ex-wife and friend, who he saw waiting in line, then killed himself.

December 20, 1997, Milwaukee, Wisconsin: Anthony DeCulit killed a coworker and wounded a supervisor and another coworker with a 9mm pistol before killing himself.

Postal Petition and Letters of Complaints

During the time when postal workers were committing mass murder, women were reporting being sexually assaulted and forced into relationships just to keep their jobs. Some of the men who complained were assaulted. These ard copies of letters and complaints sent to Congress and others asking for help.

Certified P 746 106 513

April 20, 1992

Mr. Dempsey White
Postmaster USPS
Alexandria, VA 22314

Dear Mr. White,

This is a complaint against Mr. Tracy Wade, acting supervisor, Alexandria, Va 22314, for intimidations, harassments and racial discrimination.

I have been working as a letter carrier for the last six years at this station. I am very proud of my job and I always do my work to my best effort and ability. My former customers from my former route could attest to that. There were supervisors that come and go in our station and I never had any problems with them. I am always willing to talk or accept any suggestions from the management for the improvement of the customer service.

140

Unfortunately, there will always be a rotten apple that will spoil any reputable employer-employee relationship. Ever since Mr. Tracy Wade came to our station as our supervisor, he particularly chooses me to be given an almost everyday harsh treatment. He usually nags me on my new route in which the majority of the carriers are still in their period of adjustment like me. I listened to his advice but I have to give my own suggestions because I am the actual carrier in the street. For the first few times, I dismissed his attitudes towards me as part of his job.

However, he haunts me every day, by telling me what to do. Not a neophyte myself on the job, I am always confident and very knowledgeable of my duties.

Mr. Tracy Wade's intimidations culminated on April 18, 1992, Saturday at around 7:45 in the morning. I was doing my flats when he sent somebody to do the job. So, I took my ten-minute break. When I returned to my case, I started doing my letters. Mr. Wade came and ordered me to do my letters, which I was <u>actually</u> <u>doing.</u> He repeatedly gave the same orders and even made sign language while walking away. After a few minutes, he came again giving the same order. He got a piece of paper with an arrow sign and placed it on my letters. I could really sense that he was starting his intimidations again. I remained calm and continued my letters as he wanted me to do. Later, he came again to me and ordered me to stop doing my letters and start on my flats. He even removed the piece of paper from my letters and placed it now on the flats. I asked him what he really wanted me to do or what was the game he wanted to play again on me. He told me to do exactly what he ordered and another carrier would be doing my letters.

Dear: Honorable Representative

This letter is a desperate request for your help in bringing about a full congressional investigation into the inhuman treatment of Postal Workers in Alexandria, VA. Since these matters have constantly been brought to the attention of the Alexandria, VA Postmaster Mike Harlow and the highest-ranking Postal Official in Northern VA, Mr. Curtis Weed nothing has been accomplished. It's the opinion of the

Postal Workers that the Postmaster General would never receive the complaint letters from the employees. Therefore, a response would never be answered.

.

My name Jackie Ross; while performing my duties at 136 Robert Lane, I was assaulted by my station manager Mr. Tracy Wade. Because, of Mr. Wade's history of abusive behavior toward other postal employees I was fearful for my life.

Since Mr. Wade's short period of time in Alexandria, VA, he has been involved in altercations which have led to assaults and threats. It should be noted that some employees have quit and others have been fired, but there are still a diligent number of workers who are performing their jobs under very stressful working conditions. The punishment that was given to Mr. Wade for his behaviors has been a promotion from supervisor to manager. It is now that congressional assistance is most urgent.

January 11, 1994
C. Michael Harlow Postmaster-Alexandria, VA
I, Patrice Parker, am filing a charge of sexual harassment against Memorial Annex Station Manager Tracy Wade. Tracy Wade has repeatedly made overt as well as subtle unwanted sexual advances toward me. Tracy Wade has also made several unwanted lewd remarks, gestures, and looks toward me. On one occasion he even made unwanted physical contact with me by touching me and/or putting his arm around me.

For a while I tried to ignore and avoid the unwanted sexual advances that Tracy Wade made toward me. When I kept rejecting his unwanted sexual overtures, he began to get very angry with me. Because I did not show him the special attention and adulation that some of the other women working in this station have shown him (in return for preferential treatment and/or favored work assignments and conditions),Tracy Wade began to retaliate by harassing me relentlessly at work.

142

Tracy Wade repeatedly called me into his office for discussions (often one on one with him) on the slightest infractions (for example, talking to anyone while spreading or casing the mail), that he let other individuals get by with, on an almost daily basis. When he overheard me tell a coworker how repulsive I thought he was, he literally shook with rage! That is when Tracy Wade began to act really bitter, ugly, and hateful toward me.

Tracy Wade completely took advantage of the fact that I was having severe personal problems at home (on top of all the STRESS that his numerous unwanted sexual advances at work was causing me) that were beginning to affect my attendance. When he found out that Clerk Supervisor Marty Rowles was giving me a ride to work because I didn't have a car, he ordered Marty Rowles not to pick me up anymore because it did not seem appropriate. This statement, coming from a station manager who has a young woman (Sharon Bryson), who is just an NTE casual clerk, in his own personal office all day long, doing nothing but computer work, while all the other NTE casual clerks distribute and handle mail all day long! That, clearly, does not seem appropriate to anyone except Tracy Wade!

Within just a six-month period (May 19 3-December 1993), Tracy Wade, with Marty Rowles, issued seven (count them SEVEN!) corrective actions to me concerning my attendance. For at least one year and a half until May or June of 1993 he took no action whatsoever against distribution clerk Patricia Wible, who just happens to be his close personal/girlfriend? and confidante, when she only came to work one'or two days a month for almost all of 1992 until May of 1993! I have several witnesses that can verify this because we have all been asked on several occasions to take her place when she called in on a daily basis.

GOVERNOR GEORGE ALAN,OFFICE OF GOVERNOR

FROM: NATHANIEL BLACK SR.2727 DUKE ST., #811
ALEX., VA 22314-4538
DATE: JANUARY 12, 1994

SUBJ: HARASSMENT (RETALIATION AFTER JOB-RELATED INJURY). CC: SENATOR CHARLES ROBB, SENATOR JOHN WARNER, CONGRESSMEN JAMES P. MORAN, POSTMASTER GENERAL MARVIN RUNYON, RAINBOW COALITION JESSE JACKSON, HEAD OF POSTMASTER CURTIS WEED, POSTMASTER MIKE HARLOW

DEAR GOVERNOR ALAN,

I AM WRITING THIS LETTER IN HOPE OF SEEKING SOME HELP.' I AM A LABORER/CUSTODIAN FOR THE UNITED STATES POSTAL SERVICE. I HAVE WORKED FOR THE POSTAL SERVICE FOR FIVE YEARS. TOO LONG TO BE CON-CERNED ABOUT MY JOB SECURITY. I HAVE WORKED HARD AND BEEN EXTREMELYRESPONSIBLE IN MY POSITION. I REALIZE MY RESPONSIBILITY TOWARD MY MANAGER MR. TRACY B. WADE AND THE SUPERVISORS OF MY COMMAND. I GIVE RESPECT AND FEEL THAT AS A HUMAN BEING I SHOULD RECEIVE RESPECT ALSO.
THERE HAVE BEEN NUMEROUS COMPLAINTS BROUGHT AGAINST ME THAT I FEEL ARE NOT TRUE AND UNJUST. IN PARTICULAR AN INCIDENT OCCURED RECENTLY THAT PROMPTED ME TO WRITE THIS LETTER. I WOULD LIKE TO ELABORATE ON THIS PARTICULAR MATTER.
ON SATURDAY NOVEMBER 6, 1993, I ARRIVED TO WORK EARLY (4.00AM) TO REARRANGE CASES. LATER THAT MORNING I HURT MY BACK, AND CONTINUED ON WORKING FIGURING IT WAS JUST SORE MUSCLES. MONDAY NOV.8,1993 THAT MORNING I MENTIONED IT TO SUPERVISOR MR. NORMAN COMBEST.I NEVER STOPPED WORKING. ON TUESDAY NOV. 9, 1993 # WHEN I REPORTED IT THE SECOND TIME TO SUPERVISOR MR. JAMES B. WALKER. I WILL GET TO YOU LATER WHEN I FINISH THIS REPORT. IT 6:30 AM. AT 1:15 PM IS WHEN I ARRIVED AT THE DOCTOR'S OFFICE. THE DOCTOR WAS NOT THERE. SO SUP. MR. JAMES B. WALKER MADE THE APPOINTMENT FOR THE NEXT DAY NOV. 10, 1993, AT 9:00 AM. WHEN I ARRIVED AT THE DOCTOR'S OFFICE, THE RECEPTIONIST SAID THERE WAS NOTHING ON ME. WHEN LOOKING WITH ALL DUE

144

RESPECT, I WOULD LIKE SOMEONE TO HELP ME OBTAIN A
RESOLUTION TO THIS SITUATION, AND SOME KIND OF
ACTION BROUGHT AGAINST THEM.

I SINCERELY BELIEVE THAT IF THIS STATION HAD
COMPETENT LEADERSHIP, THERE WOULD HAVE BEEN NO
NEED FOR THIS LETTER

RESPECTFULLY YOURS

Nathaniel Black Jr.

Congressional Black Caucus
c/o s. Amelia Parker, Executive Director Room 344
Ford House Office Building Washington, D.C. 20515

Dear Ms. Parker:

I am an employee of the Alexandria Division of the United States
Postal Service. My concern is with the status of my future
employment with this federal agency. My hope is that you will bring a
prompt and complete halt to the Dred Scott type behavior that is
forever present in this division of the C.S. Postal Service.

In Alexandria, Virginia, employees are treated as if they have no
rights that this agency should slightly consider respecting, so they do
not post adverse disciplinary actions have victimized only the
African-American employees. Of the nearly 50 employee
terminations in this city since 1985, all but a few have fallen on the
necks of African- Americans.

We invite you to conduct your disparity study since we know that
such a study would confirm all of the above. In conclusion, we ask
that you order this agency to immediately cease and desist with its
present mode of operation and to align itself with present day EEOC
rules and regulations and all other corrective actions embodied in the
legislature.

Sincerely,

<u>Comparable</u> <u>Incidents of Assaults, Threats and Altercations in</u> <u>Alexandria, Virginia</u>

1. In October 1990, Angel Beard and Julie Dybus had threatening altercations on both the workroom floor and the loading dock.

2. In October 1990, several employees, including a supervisor, were involved with employee, Angel Beard, in exchanging sexual favors for drugs while falsifying clock rings and delaying the mail to do so. No employees were disciplined in reference to these outrageous incidents even though Ms. Beard informed both the union and management that she felt threatened to exchange her sexually with the many employees involved. She was merely sent to another postal station and management took no corrective action.

3. In December 1990, employee Phil Gurrie assaulted employee Felicia Byrd.

4. In December 1990, employee Donna Andre assaulted employee Florence A, Haynes.

5. In December 1990, employee Donna Andre created an altercation with employee Jackie Burrous-Springs.

6. In January 1991, postal employee, Shirley Greer stopped performing her mail processing duties and left the postal premise, without authorization, to follow a male postal customer who had come to pick up mail for his employer, Household Goods at 1611 Duke Street, Alexandria, Va.
Once she arrived at is place of employment, Ms, Green propositioned the customer for sexual favors. The customer, in turn, reported the incident to his superior who then informed the U.S. Postal Service, Alexandria, Va. No corrective action was ever taken on this matter.

7. In February 1991, employee Donald Kirby made racial remarks to employee Ella Wise. ·

8. In early March 1991, employee John Goodrich had a threatening altercation with supervisor Tracy Wade on the workroom floor. Wade

ordered Goodrich into the office where the threatening altercation continued.

9. In March 1991, during a workroom floor meeting, employee Betty Crawford informed the Manager of Customer Service, Shoshana Grove, that she had been repeatedly threatened by station manager Donna Sager,

10. In March 1991, employee Donald Kirby threatened supervisor Walter Stewart and a customer.

'11. On March 19, 1991, supervisor Tracey Wade twice assaulted employee Ronald M. Lewis.

12. In April 1991, employee Phil Gurrie cursed employee Betty Crawford twice in one day.

13. On April 15, 1991, employee Phil Gurrie and customer service manager Shoshana Grove were involved in a threatening altercation.

14. In May 1991, station manager Donna Sager and employee Steve Fields had a threatening altercation.

15. In July 1991, employee Vincent Cunning and employee Donald Lotimaker had a threatening altercation.

16. In July 1991, customer service manager Shoshana Grove and supervisor Walter Stewart had a threatening altercation.

17. In July 1991, customer service manager Shoshana Grove and supervisor Barbara Williams had a threatening altercation.

18. In September 1991, supervisor Walter Swobota and employee Michael Ross were fighting on the workroom floor.

19. On September 9, 1991, supervisor Tracey Wade created a threatening altercation with employee Larry Colbert.

20. In November 1991, supervisor Tracey Wade threatened employee Richard Salizar.

21. In November 1991, customer service manager Shoshana Grove and supervisor Walter Stewart had a threatening altercation.

22. On November 13, 1991, employee Terry Arnold sexually harassed customers on his route at the Carlson TravelNetwork, which is located at 635 Slater Lane in Alexandria, Va.

23. On January 2, 1992, employee Terry Arnold used force in order to kiss employee Krystal Galloway on her lips.

24.   On January 6, 1992, supervisor Tracey Wade created a loud workroom floor altercation with employee Steve Fields.

25. On January 7, 1992, supervisor Tracey Wade repeatedly threatened employee Edmond Wright.

26. On February 3, 1992, supervisor Tracey Wade threatened employee Larry Colbert.

27. On February 24, 1992, supervisor Tracey Wade threatened employee Gary Bean.

28. On February 25, 1992, supervisor Frank Gushost threatened employee Lanny Newman.

29. On March 7, 1992, supervisor Donna Andre threatened employee Jackie Ross.

30. On March 9, 1992, supervisor Donna Andre threatened employee Larry Colbert.

31. In April 1992, employee George Smallfield threatened to bring an Uzi machine pistol to the workroom floor and kill everybody.

32. On April 9, 1992, employee Terry Arnold loudly threatened to

bring his guns onto the workroom floor to settle his financial problems with the management.

33. On April 18, 1992, supervisor Tracey Wade was the subject of a discrimination complaint filed by employee Allyson Bustimonte.

34. On April 25, 1992, customer service manager Shoshana Grove created a threatening altercation with employee Mary Hoffman.

35. In May 1992, supervisors Norman Combest and Walter Stewart were charged with the sexual harassment of employee Ella Wise.

36. On July 6, 1992, supervisor Frank Gushost created a threatening altercation with employee Lanny Newman.

37. On July 27, 1992, Alexandria Postmaster, Dempsey White, used loud, abusive and disrespectful language towards employee Larry Colbert. On the same day, station manager Sam Rodriques cursedemployee Ella Wise on the workroom floor.

39. On July 27, 1992, supervisor, Frank Gushot, disrespected employee, Maurice Cleveland, by calling him a black boy.

40. On July 28, 1992, supervisor Frank Gushot was loud, abusive and disrespectful to employee Ella Wise.

41. In August 1992, supervisor Frank Gushot assaulted employee Kyle Lawrence.

42. On August 31, 1992, employee Mary Hoffman was harassed repeatedly and forced off the clock by supervisor, Frank Gushot.

43. On September 21, 1992, an emergency call came in to the annex station for employee John Sherman because his daughter had been hit by a car. Postal officials refused to contact the employee even after two additional calls were made by Prince George's County Police. Mr. Sherman's daughter died after about one hour and he did not learn of it until his wife came on his route

to tell him. On the next day, Frank Gushot, the supervisor who had received the emergency call, was transferred to Lincolnia Station. Employees of that station engaged in a work stoppage and refused his supervision as an expression of their disapproval of his actions against Mr. Sherman.

44. On or about January 12, 1993, supervisor Norman Combestand Mark Picciano were involved in an early morning threatening altercation.

45. On January 23, 1993, employee Donald Kirby threatened the life of employee John Sherman without provocation.

46. On March 11, 1993, a Caucasian employee, John Kowal, told an Afro-American female employee, Laura Gamble, that he wanted her to suck his penis.

150

The Ku Kolored Klan

In a speech given while he was the minister of the Dexter Avenue Baptist Church, Dr. Martin Luther King spoke of the toll that hate takes on the individual of the group who hates. He ended his speech by saying: "...There is nothing more tragic than a person whose heart is filled with hate." The hate Dr. King spoke of has come home to claim the people he tried to save from hate.

It is only because African Americans are descendants of tribal people that we as a group can be saved from the actions of the majority in our race. I say this because African Americans will follow leaders, good and bad. There is hope, that is, if a savior can manipulate the abortion and murder maze and be born. Until then, the Woke African American majority should be accepted as the people replacing the Ku Klux Klan as the military wing of the Democrat Party.

Woke African Americans' obsession with racism they have never experienced or done anything about doesn't make them a little bit racist; it made them hard-core racists. One needs only to look back in time at the history of the Ku Klux Klan to understand that the two histories and mission have merged. Like the Klan, the African American Democrat majority exist to serve the political needs of the party that created them.

Make no mistake about the source of African Americans' hatred for Republicans, Conservatives, and those they disagree with. This particular kind of hatred was not born out of racism or mistreatment but politics. Otherwise, they would hate White Southern Democrats. Therefore, the source cannot be racism because they support the works of Margaret Sanger.

This hatred, bitterness, and willingness to be pawns can be traced back to the election of Barack Obama as President. Just when racism was on its deathbed, the ghost of racism manifested in the form of Massa's child. President Obama did nothing for African Americans other than leave the Black race with a legacy of hate that created a Ku Kolored Klan.

If one were to ask a Klansman why they hate Black people, they would deny it, perhaps by saying they don't hate Black people; they just love White people more. The Ku Kolored Klan does the same thing in reverse. They don't hate White people; White people hate Black people.

Most African American know they are wrong, but the fear of reprisal from within the African American community keeps most African American in line. Consider this. As loyal as African American Democrats are on Election Day, most are ashamed of being

Democrats. I have gotten into arguments with African Americans who always vote straight Democrat tickets. They never have anything good to say about any Republican. Yet, they will bring up their voter registration and argue they are independent. They never use the merits of the Democrat Party when condemning Conservatives and other Black people who don't toe the line.

It is almost impossible to find an African American who openly supports the Democrat Party by name. Nor will one hear or read about African Americans saying anything good about the Democrat Party. On social media during an election one may see something like "Riding with Biden" or Obama is the best President ever, but that's about it. You will not find requests asking people to become Democrats. This is why they always claim the parties switched. The only time they publicly defend Democrats is in the abstract tally coming out of the voting booth.

In the privacy of the voting booth, Woke African Americans do horrible and unjust things to our culture and race. Our ancestors, who died fighting for voting rights, never dreamed their sacrifices would be a curse. The KKK and Neo Nazis cannot match what African American Democrats do to the Black race on Election Day. I learned a lot more about what hate does to the individual from African Americans than I did in six years of employment with White Southern racists and Klansmen.

Today the God-inspired Christian Abolitionist along with Abraham Lincoln, and almost 400,000 Union soldiers who died to free Black people are vilified and disrespected. They are so hate-filled, the hate has become part of their psyche. Because their hate is taught rather than a learned behavior from mistreatment, African Americans see everyone they disagree with as someone that hates them. They believe anything the Republican Party does is bad, and anything Democrats do is good. Although it was Democrats who enslaved and lynched Black people, the hate will not allow African Americans to comprehend it was the Democrats' doing.

African Americans claim the Republican Party is too racist to join. Yet, they joined the Democrat Party while Democrats were segregating and lynching Black people. Rather than defend voting for Democrats, they will claim the parties switched and continue to the polls in record numbers. While they were at the polls, they voted for Southern segregationist Dixiecrats like Wallace, Long, and Byrd. These were White Supremacists who caused an untold amount of suffering and death of Black people. However, Black people like me with a civil rights and social justice history cannot find room in their hearts.

To support my charges, I have documented the complicity of those Dr. King said were insensitive to the masses' needs because of a degree of academic success. I have also documented cases of retaliation, and persecution, at the hands of those Dr. King referred to as "drained of self-respect." Combined, those Opposing Forces in the Black community have allowed Corporate America, the media, race hustlers, and the Left to cloak their agenda in Kente Cloth and exploit and manipulate the Black community for generations. The self-hate has suppressed Black America's survival instincts to a level where lives do not matter. We see this in the mission of Black Lives Matter. They rose up with a name wrapped in a mission that somehow, amid an abortion, suicide, and murder epidemic, seems like it is asking a question rather than valuing lives.

I copied some of the nicer comments from my Facebook page to back my charges. From their comments, one can get to know the type of people who constructed racism, created the Klan, and used that expertise to turn African Americans into a hate group. To bring out the worst hate from those making comments, I only had to prove I have a civil rights record. In their minds, they cannot imagine or accept that a Conservative can earn a civil rights record.

To aid in reading these comments, Names were deleted with the exception of Dee Wash. Dee name is not deleted because Dee is a public person.

Facebook Comments

Jimmy Pratt: *MS writer and producer. No wonder I've never watched a single episode of* the wire. *Heard it won an Emmy, not surprised.*
Dee Wash: It won the following:
Peabody Award
TCA Heritage award…

Dee Wash so your ignorance is intentional all in the name of your damn book? I'm writing a script and I have to write in a character based on you....this is too good
Also... last I checked I'm a free woman... you're the one enslaved with a weak mental…

Mr. Jimmy hates his race so much he blames them for damn near everything... What proof does he have to back up his ridiculous assertion? NONE... he aligns the KKK with blacks in an attempt to show exactly what?

Mr. Jimmy once again ignores the WHITE faces of those who actually committed the crimes mentioned in the article he posted on his page and IN HIS INFINITE SO CALLED SUPERIOR KNOWLEDGE he chooses to blame blacks instead.
Why do you hate your own race so much boy?

Jimmy Pratt I'm the brainwashed one? Carry on with your ignorance of me... Your display of assigning blame to blacks is in full display no matter how you try to spin it.
Question... what color are African Americans?
BLACK...
YOU assigned race in your attempt to blame a race of people which you have cast to the side....
You just CLEARLY stated that your personal emotional attachment to issues relating to you have clouded your judgement against your own race...
Get the f*ck outta here with your lame ass. This isn't about you... it's fie the greater good of a race you once were a part of. Carry on... boy.

Jimmy Pratt also FACT the KKK hates your black ass also... oh, wait... I notice you conveniently left that out trying to prove a one-sided point.
You're not one of us

Jimmy Pratt What's your definition of "Black Liberal"? What's your source on this narrow opinion? In addition, what is the source of your hatred of black people?

Jimmy Pratt: oh and fuck you, didn't want to forget that part, now scoot along with your hate filled, soul sucking, tick sized brain and have a good weekend

Jimmy Pratt you're so godamn dumb that you call the use of words that are in the English language plagiarism............... So are we supposed to make up our own words now? Why do we have dictionaries and thesauruses if we aren't supposed to use t
Jimmy Pratt: ...and Cuomo was not the only one guilty of putting Ccovid-19 patients in nursing homes where the already infirm were at risk. It happened in every state blue and red so suck on that along with

the artificial dick your drooling over

Summary

The politics of the African American majority has led to a race of people becoming servants. Like Canaan in the Bible, African American Democrats exist only to serve the Left and the Democrat Party.

As I close this book, the Kyle Rittenhouse trial comes to mind and the outrage of African Americans over the death of two White criminals. This too is a testament to the real-life events that created this book. The African American majority who have the political power to change the destiny of Black children and their communities are frozen in President Johnson's prediction of "Niggers" voting Democrat for 100 years and therefore unable to care.

Self-preservation is the First Law of Nature until African American's Democrat go to the polls. Everything from unlawful mandates, to supporting atheists, to destroying churches, to COVID mandates, to illegal immigration, to unlawfully locking up people... these were all made possible in the name of equity and equality for

Black people. For their contributions to wokeness, African Americans did not gain anything other than a platform from which to call people racist. In the meantime, Black kids can't read at grade level and are drowning in their own blood.

The African American History of suffering is the Left's moral justification for all the evil they do. With that history, the Left uses racism to create remedies for Black people that serves them. But, somehow, those remedies keep getting applied to other people and causes like trans and immigrants.

The Left talks of justice, but the evidence is clear. They do not want civil rights laws enforced or protest to stop. They want and need a permanent Black underclass who not only believe everything is racist but do not know the value of their vote. This gift to the Left is used to change everything except the conditions the Left keep the Black race locked in.

The 2020 election gave power to the Left, and they wasted no time using it. In May of 2021, the Left canceled a 16-year-old American Idol contestant for being in a photo with a person with a hood on but left Ralph Narthram alone. This may all seem insignificant when compared to other cases in this book, including the fake investigation, the fake news release sent out by the NCDOC, the murder of Joyce Sinclaire, the cover-up of it all by the MSM, A&E, and NBC.

However, everything the Left and their African American puppets did to us and others was the groundwork for something much larger. What they did in the name of fighting racism led to troops at the Capitol defunding the police, and countless Executive Orders. Unless Conservative Christians stand up to the Left, they will never suffer the consequences of their racist actions and we will lose a country.

Conservative Christians should use the information in this book to hold progressive and liberals accountable for their acts of racism against the Black race in America. Christian Conservatives should follow the example set by the Democrats and take no prisoners. Conservatives should call out the people, even from the grave, for issuing a fake News Release. Conservatives should demand an immediate investigation into the racist murder of Joyce Sinclair and expose the press and civil rights leaders who covered up her murder.

Neither BLM, nor the NAACP, nor any civil rights groups over the decades advocated using local, state, and federal anti-discrimination agencies or laws to combat racism. Nor do they demand free lawyers for victims of discrimination, whereas victims of workplace discrimination were once given free lawyers to sue. Rather than help Black people obtain attorneys, these organizations ignore all the civil rights laws people died for and choose to protest instead. The Left knows if the voices of the victims of racism are heard in court, it would not take long for elected leaders, civil rights organizations, the press, and the DNC to become obsolete.

FBI REPORT

This is one of several complaints that I filed with the Justice Department. I filed these complaints on behalf of Black officers and inmates as well.

USA, Greensboro, N.

CE 44A-4122 Bureau File
SUPERINTENDENT BRUCE E. MARION,
MOORE COUNTY PRISON UNIT,
NORTH CAROLINA DEPARTMENT OF CORRECTION,
CARTHAGE, NORTH CAROLINA.
UNKNOWN VICTIMS
CIVIL RIGHTS

In a letter dated 3/17/83, JIMMY PRATT, Pinehurst, N. C., advised that Captain MARION beat and framed inmates and then took warrants out on them. PRATT made other non-brutality allegations against Captain MARION. Upon interview, PRATT advised that Captain MARION never physically beat any inmates, only arranging to cover up beatings by his Correctional Officer One incident involved an Indian male, and the other incident involved a SHERMAN WALL. PRATT advised that he was formerly a Correctional Officer under the supervision of Captain MARION and was terminated on 3/6/83 for negligence in performance of duty and refusal to accept a reasonable and proper assignment. Personnel records, North Carolina Department of Correction, revealed PRATT was dismissed on 3/5/83 for negligence in performance of duties, and refusal to accept a reasonable and proper assignment from an authorized Supervisor (primarilyinsubordination.

CE 44A-41222

JIMMY (NO MIDDLE NAME) PRATT,
Pinehurst, North Carolina, mailing address General Delivery, Pinehurst, North Carolina, Residence Route 1, Box 32A, Eagle Springs, North Carolina, residence telephone number 673-0558, was advised of the identity of the interviewing Agent and the nature of the inquiry.

PRATT advised that he was employed as a Correctional Officer from January 18, 1979, to March 6, 1983, at the Moore County Unit of the North Carolina Department of Correction, Carthage, North Carolina. PRATT advised that his employment was terminated on March 6, 1983, for negligence in the performance of duty and refusal to accept reasonable and proper assignment for supervision.

PRATT advised that on January 24, 1983, Sergeant HEW MARTINDALE, Correctional Officer at the North Carolina

Department of Correction, Moore County Unit, Carthage, North Carolina, told him to go to Post Number Three, which is a tower. PRATT advised MARTINDALE that he would go as soon as he went to the canteen to get a soda and something to eat. PRATT advised that on his return from the canteen to the office, he decided why should he have to go to the tower at post three because he knew that Captain BRUCE HARIOH's friend, Johnny COLE, is presently assigned to the tower and COLE receives special favors for working in the tower. He gets weekends off and holidays also off.

PRATT advised that while he was discussing going to the tower with Sergeant MARTINDALE, Captain MARION came up and asked what was going on, and he stated that he wanted to know why he had to go to Post Number Three and Captain MARION said because you were told to do so. PRATT then asked Captain MARION how long, and Captain MARION yelled at him, "until you are relieved."

PRATT advised that the reason that correctional Officer COLE gets special favors for working Tower Number Three is because there is no water and no bathroom located in the tower.

PRATT advised that during this discussion with captain MARION and Sergeant MARTINDALE, Captain MARION said, "You are

PRATT' advised that the reason he questioned going to Tower Number Three was that there were some new guards in training from a new prison unit at Troy, North Carolina, and he felt like it was punishment for him, BOBBY PERSON and NORMAN MANESS, the other black Correctional Officers, to have to go to Tower Number. Three when there were new trainees available. PRATT advised that he felt that anytime that he was put on a tower, it was punishment, or if they put you there twice in the same day. He stated there are three towers at the Moore County Correctional Unit, one on the front and one behind the sewing plant, and one near the ball field in the back of the prison. He stated that Mr. COLE, who works Tower Number Three, only gets a half hour break during the day.

PRATT advised that he works first shift from 6 a.m. to 2 n.m. and Tower Number Three is manned from 6:30 a.m. to 4 pm, five days per week while work is being done in the· sewing plant. He stated that COLE mans the tower from 6:30 to 2:30 and then second shift Correctional Officers handle the tower until 4 pm when the sewing plant is closed.

PRATT advised that Captain MARION treats all black Officers and black inmates as animals. He stated that Captain MARION refers to blacks as "niggers," and has admitted this to Assistant Secretary MOONEHAM, North Carolina Department of Correction, Raleigh, North Carolina, and to ROBERT MATTHEWS, Investigator for the Employee Relations, State Personnel Office, Raleigh, North Carolina.

PRATT advised that about two years ago, at about 8:30 one evening, an inmate, an Indian, (FIRST NAME UNKNOWN), last name believed to be HUNT, age 35-36, an epileptic who had a handlebar mustache broke a lot of windows out of the sick room at the Moore County Unit.

PRATT advised that the Correctional Officers were counting the population of inmates at this time and when they finished, Sergeant HOWIE and Officer TERRY STREETER went to the Sergeant's Office and got a slapjack and a riot baton and returned to the sick room where the Indian male was hiding behind a bed. He stated that he stayed in the hall and Sergeant HOWIE and Officer STREETER drug the inmate from behind the bed and beat him. PRATT advised that he could see them beating the Indian male.

PRATT advised that Captain MARION had the Correctional Officers who were involved make statements in favor of STREETER and HOWIE.

CE 44A-4122   3 3

PRATT advised that he made a statement that the Indian male HUNT was breaking out windows and acting in an irrational· manner and that he called Supervisor JOHNNY FRYE. PRATT advised that he feels that Captain MARION let the above incident happen and covered it up by having the Officers make statements in favor of the Correctional Officers and shipped all the inmate witnesses out to other units.

PRATT advised that Correctional Officer BOBBY PRESSLER wrote a statement concerning the Indian male's beating in favor of Sergeant HOWIE, and Officer STREETER. He stated that he wanted to go help Officer HOWIE and STREETER but they told him that he could not go in and he had to stay in the hall.

PRATT advised that inmates JAMES COLLINS, REGINALD FAIRLEY, and another unknown inmate, were witnesses to the assault on the Indian male and were transferred out.
. .
PRATT advised that Captain MARION got warrants at the Moore County Courthouse charging the Indian male with assault on officers and destruction of state property. He said he felt it was an unfair conviction as Captain MARION did not let any of the Officers go. He and one of the Sergeants were present at the hearing and the Indian male got an additional six months sentence after a plea bargain agreement.   ..

PRATT advised that about four or five months ago in the sewing plant, SHERMAN WALL, an inmate, was working during his serving time at the Moore County Unit, was waiting to get out on parole. He stated that Captain MARION came to WALL in the sewing plant, and in a nasty way· told WALL he was not going anywhere because a detainer had been received from Florida and Captain MARION left the sewing plant.   ·

PRATT advised that ARTHUR (LAST NAME UNKNOWN), a Supervisor in the sewing plant, then began harassing WALL and WALL told the Supervisor to leave him alone, and when the Supervisor continued to harass WALL about not getting out of prison, WALL jumped up with a pair of scissors in his hand and told the Supervisor if he did not leave him alone, he would stick the scissors in him.

PRATT advised that WALL was locked up in the sick room and then shipped out to another prison unit. He stated that WALL was later charged with attempted murder on Supervisor ARTHUR (LAST NAME UNKNOWN) and was tried in the Moore County Courthouse, Carthage, North Carolina.

CE 44A-4122 4

PRATT advised that there are other incidents in which Captain MARION has been involved. Be stated that MICHAEL MCLEAN, an inmate, wanted a transfer to a prison unit near his home, and Captain MARION placed him in the sick room and would not let him out for about a month.

PRATT advised that LACEY BUTLER was locked up for a··. sprained ankle which he received while playing basketball because he could not go to work.

He stated that (FIRST NAME UNKNOWN) PEARSALL, an inmate, was locked up in the sick room for not going to work.

PRATT advised that Captain MARION refuses to pay overtime or give time off for overtime hours. He stated that in emergency situations, Correctional Officers are called into work. He stated he has worked about 30 times during his employment over time and has not been paid for about 200 hours. He stated that Captain MARION would not let Correctional Officers see their timesheets. He stated that overtime occurs when an inmate is taken to a funeral and on an occasion he had to go to a riot at the Columbus County Unit of the North Carolina Department of Correction and put in overtime.

PRATT stated that to become a member of the State Employee's Association, he had to pay to join and Captain MARION would not let him attend the meetings or would not announce the meetings, and Captain MARION would handpick people to attend the State Employee's Association meetings.

PRATT advised that promotions were only given to those persons who were related in a clique from the Moore County Unit.

PRATT advised that Captain MARION refused to let LACEY BUTLER get medical attention and BUTLER used the excuse that he needed to go then to the law library at the McCain Unit of the North Carolina Department of Correction and then when he got to McCain, BUTLER got medical attention. He stated that BUTLER now has a civil suit against Ms. (FIRST NA. UNKNOWN) BRYANT the Moore County Unit Nurse.

PRATT advised that black Correctional Officer BOBBY PERSON said that Nurse BRYANT refused to treat BUTLER.

CE 44A-4122 5

PRATT advised that Captain MARION's wife works at Phillips Motor Company in Carthage, which is the Ford dealer on Highway 15 and 501 across from the Moore County Board of Education, and Phillips is on the Advisory Committee to the prison and he feels this is a conflict of interest. He stated that Phillips also does work on state vehicles.

PRATT advised that Captain MARION has paid someone to bring truckloads of dirt to the Moore County Prison Unit out of state funds and was intending to make a ballfield, however, has done nothing with it and there are trees growing out of the dirt which has been dumped and left laying near the ballpark.

PRATT advised that he feels that the authorities in Raleigh, North Carolina, in the North Carolina Department of_ Correction are looking out for Captain MARION as two Lieutenants at the McCain Unit of the North Carolina Department of Correction got fired for doing a beating on an inmate and if Captain MARION gets involved in something, it is covered up.

PRATT advised that if an inmate gets a charge against Captain MARION, arrangements are made to get the inmate out of prison.

166

PRATT advised that inmate LARRY STRADER got out of prison because the FBI investigated a case. He stated that Captain MARION tried to get STRADER to say that Guard MARCUS WADSWORTH, Moore County Unit, ate steaks which were missing from the kitchen of the prison unit, and when he refused STRADER was charged with the theft of the steaks.

PRATT advised that he made a complaint to TONY CAULDER, the Equal Employment Opportunity Commission, Charlotte, North Carolina, telephone number 704/371-6450, against Captain MARION and the North Carolina Department of Correction for discrimination in promotions, mining and hiring of black personnel..

PRATT advised that sometime in 1982, ALBERT SILER, a black inmate, was refused medical treatment on three different occasions when he was beaten by inmates. PRATT advised that SILER begged for medical treatment and it was refused. SILER was assaulted by ANTHONY JOHNSON and SILER was refused to see a doctor for five days.

PRATT advised that the Honor Grade committee which declares inmates to honor grade classification is made up of the Program Supervisor and two Correctional Officers, and it is stacked up against black inmates. He stated that two....... ago, DAVE MIREE, a white inmate, got out of segregation.......... to honor grade. He stated at the same time, black inmate (FIRST NAME UNKNOWN) PERSALL and others were refused honor grade classification.

PRATT advised that Correctional Officer JERRY LEWIS, a Road Crew Officer, points guns at inmates and this is the reason why a lot of inmates will not work on the road.

PRATT advised that black inmate JOSEPH LILLY got an eye hurt while working on the road, and the eye was almost put out and he was made to work all day long on the road crew and did not get brought back to the unit for medical attention until the end of the workday.

PRATT advised that he has never known Captain MARION to hit an

167

inmate, but he feels that Captain MARION covers up and frames inmates when struck by Correctional Officers.

PRATT advised that he got sick of the treatment that was being given to the inmates at the Moore County Unit of the North Carolina Department of Correction at Carthage, North Carolina, and made a complaint to DWIGHT SANDERFORD, FRANK GUNTER, and JOE HAMILTON in the Headquarters of the North Carolina Department of Correction at Raleigh.

PRATT advised that in about November of 1981, a white inmate, (FIRST NAME UNKNOWN) SHEFFIELD, a known racist to prison officials, was sent to the Moore County Unit. PRATT advised that SHEFFIELD tricked a black inmate to come to the back of the prison and SHEFFIELD cut the black inmate with a straight razor. PRATT advised that as a general rule, individuals who have a history of being racist and assaulting blacks are kept in single cell units. PRATT further stated that they already had racial problems at the Moore_ County Unit, and sending in this inmate who had a racist background, did not make sense.

The following is a description of Pratt
Race Negro

NCDOC Investigation Recommendations

It is hard in this day and time to believe this is still being covered up by people tearing down Confederate flags, renaming streets and military post in the name of social justice. However, it fits well with today's racial narrative. In order to be expose, the man who wrote this report and did the investigation needed to be White.

(1)   That the North Carolina Department of Correction administer appropriate disciplinary action against Superintendent Marion for using inappropriate and racially derogatory language in the past ("Nigger") toward another State employee.

(2)   That the North Carolina Department of Correction take appropriate disciplinary measures toward any employee found bringing materials or documents that are of a racist or racially derogatory nature.

(3)   That Correctional Officer Eddie Lane be strongly considered for promotion to the next Sergeant vacancy at the Unit. That on-the-job training be given to enhance promotability of minority employees.

(4)   That Respondent intervene to determine that Correctional Officer Larry Cates is not supervised by Sergeant Archie Peele to avoid violating State personnel policy against nepotism.

(5)   That all Correctional Officers at the Moore County facility be reminded that any discussion of the current problems with the News Media should be cleared by the Superintendent first. That they always follow the chain of command.

That all qualified Correctional Officers at the Moore County Unit be encouraged to take the Sergeants examination.

Robert H. Mathes
Investigator

March 29, 1983, cc: Mrs. Juanita Baker
Mr. Bobby Mooneyham
Mr. Jimmy Pratt
Mr. Bobby Person

Court Cases

These are just a portion of the court case Bobby and I were involved in. In addition to the court case there were EEOC investigations. All of the EEOC investigations were turned over to minorities who could not find discrimination even when it was admitted.

BOBBY PERSON,   JIMMY PRATT
V.
NORTH CAROLINA DEPARTMENT OF CORRECTIONS
-
BOBBY L. PERSON, individually and on behalf of all others similarly situated,
plaintiff
V.
CAROLINA KNIGHTS OF THE KU KLUX KLAN, an unincorporated association
BOBBY PERSON, JIMMIE PRATT, HILTON DUNLAP, WILTON C DUNLAP,
PHILLIP McMillan, HOSEA BROWER, and ZEBULON GORDON
V.
MOORE COUNTY BOARD OF COMMISSIONERS; MOORE COUNTY
BOARD OF EDUCATION; MOORE COUNTY BOARD of ELECTIONS; and
TOWN COUNCIL of SOUTHERN PINES, NORTH CAROLINA
-
CONCERNED CITIZENS OF MOORE COUNTY and JIMMY PRATT
V.

TOWN OF TAYLORTOWN and GENEVA McRae, FRANCIS JACKSON, DAN MORRISON, and LARRY ALFORD, individually and in their official capacity as members of the Taylortown Board

JIMMY PRATT
V,
TOWN of TAYLORTOWN

-

JAMES PRATT
V,
MONUMENTAL PAPER COMPANY

-

JIMMY PRATT
V,
WALMER ENTERPRISES, INC

Boards
North Carolinians Against Racist And Religious Violence

Fairfax County Community Advisory Board
Founding member of Voices for Justice

Made in the USA
Middletown, DE
10 October 2023